MW00788523

U.S. ARMY INSIGNIA
1941-45

Volume one: Army groups,
Armies, Army corps, Infantry Divisions

Pierre BESNARD

HISTOIRE & COLLECTIONS

INTRODUCTION

United States Army shoulder patches constitute an extremely interesting collecting theme that does not require a lot of space and which is affordable for most collectors.

Dating from the First World War, these two 81st US Infantry Division shoulder patches can be considered as being the first of this type of insignia used by the US Army. On the left, the black wildcat has been roughly cut out and sewn onto a circular piece of khaki cloth. On the right is a more elaborate pattern.
(Coll. ASMIC)

The demise of bright-colored uniforms at the beginning of the 20th century, where each regiment, arm or service wore its own colours, was not without consequence to 'esprit de corps.' The British innovated in WWI by wearing, on standard brown colored uniforms, cloth insignia sewn onto the service coat sleeves. These were at first simply made and comprised of a geometric shape, then with a more elaborate design, such as symbols related to the region from which the soldiers of the division were recruited.

In the United States no such thing was planned for. During the Civil War and the Spanish-American War, basic colour insignia was attached to headwear to identify army corps and divisions, symbols which foreshadowed the shoulder patches of 1918.

In April 1918, Major-General Charles J. Bailey, commanding the 81st Division at Camp Jackson, sent out a memorandum that announced his intention to create a divisional sign, adding that all suggestions were welcome. It was Captain Florence who put forward the famous wildcat symbolizing the Wildcat creek area of South Carolina, where the division was raised. This insignia would be worn on uniforms and painted on vehicles, tents and baggage. This version was adopted by Bailey on 24 May 1918. An order for 60,000 patches was placed with the Cote Bros. and Kennedy company, specifying that they had to be delivered before the division left for France, something that was due for the first week of August. Whilst embarking at Hoboken (New Jersey), the men of the 81st Div., with their wildcat patch sewn at the top of the left sleeve, did not go unnoticed by sharp eye of the officer in command of the port who, given such a flagrant flouting of regulations, reported the incident to Washington. This would fall on deaf ears, as later events went on to prove.

Indeed, as soon as they arrived in France, the 81st Division patch was so well-received that all the divisions of the American Expeditionary Force wanted to have their own distinctive insignia. An AEF General-Staff memo dated 18 October 1918 authorized the definitive adoption, for each large unit, of a shoulder sleeve insignia. By the summer of 1919 there were more than 80 patterns that had been approved. The design of these insignia were extremely varied, but one could often find, stylized or not, the unit's number or a symbol representing where the unit was activated. However, the wearing of the shoulder patch remained forbidden in the USA, even for men returning from Europe, and it was not until May 1920 that they were officially recognized.

The symbols of 1918-19 remained present on the insignia of the Second World War divisions and on those that are still active today.

The manufacture and identification of shoulder patches

During the Second World War, using a procedure that was developed in the nineteen-thirties, the patches were machine embroidered onto wide sections of cotton that were then cut into strips before the patches were cut out individually. Regulation patches were ordered from a multitude of civilian manufacturers working under contract, following patterns supplied by the US Army, some examples of which are seen opposite. There are, however, variations in the embroidery, depending on the manufacturer.

The exact dating of patches is not straightforward as many units remained active after 1945 and the manufacturing process was only changed for the first time in 1966 (see following page).

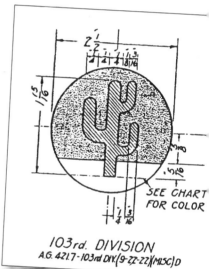

103rd. DIVISION
A.G. 421.7-103rd DIV (9-22-22)(MISC.) D

We should also retain the fact that, for the period of 1940-45, many units procured patches locally. One can find, therefore, within the ETO, British, Italian, French, Belgian and even German-made patches. Of course, these patches often include differences with the original pattern, as much in texture as in the colour tones and graphics. Finally, it should be mentioned that theatre made bullion patches were not regulation and their wearing was forbidden by the adjutant general, something which did not, of course, prevent them from being worn…

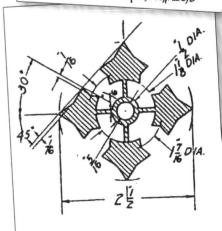

FOURTH DIVISION
A.G.A.E.F. OCT. 30, 1918.
A.G. 421.7-4th.DIV (6-20-22)(MISC.) 4.

The evolution of the 2nd Division patch, 1930-2009

With this example of this very well known patch, we illustrate the different types of manufacture of the same patch from 1930 to today (the dates given are a guideline), what is valid for this division is of course also valid for all the others.

1 Embroidered Indian head on a white felt star that is itself sewn onto black felt (1930-35).
2 Indian head and star embroidered onto black felt (1930-35).
3 Indian head and star embroidered onto twill (1935-40).
4 Entirely embroidered pattern with olive drab edging (1940-45).
5 Entirely embroidered pattern without edging (1940-68).
6 Entirely embroidered pattern with merrowed border (1968 to today).
7 Subdued patch: Indian head embroidered onto an olive drab star which is itself sewn onto a black star, one of the numerous variations of this pattern (1966-68).
8 Entirely embroidered subdued patch, olive drab star on a black star with standard border (1966-68).
9 Entirely embroidered subdued patch, olive drab star on a black star with merrowed border (1968-2004).
10 Desert subdued with merrowed border (also a theatre made version embroidered on twill, Turkish or Iraqi, 1991-2004).
11 Army Combat Uniform (ACU) patch, generally sewn onto a piece of velcro ™ (2005-today).

Contrary to a common idea spread by numerous authors, including ourselves, patches with olive drab or khaki edges do not come from Army embroidery workshops as such a thing did not exist. The explanation is much more straightforward and this photo shows the reason for OD or khaki edges on some 1940-45 patches. Before this period, patches were mainly embroidered onto olive drab wool for winter garments, and on khaki cloth for summer garments. With the advent of patches fully embroidered on twill, some manufacturers delivered patches with an olive drab border for the winter uniform and a khaki (tan) border for the summer outfit. This matched the colours of the spools of thread supplied to soldiers in their sewing kits, together with a spool of white cotton thread for repairing underwear, that was generally white at the beginning of the war.

How to date an American patch?

At the end of the nineteen-thirties, American patches were machine embroidered onto a backing that was generally tan-colored cotton.

This type of patch coexisted with patches embroidered on wool, felt or twill.

Starting in 1940, and approximately up to 1943, many fully embroidered patches had an olive drab or khaki border (see page 5).

In 1955, the U.S. Army decided to replace the olive drab "victory uniform" with a more modern design uniform in Army Green 44. The backing or border of some patches thus became dark green.

From approximately 1966 onwards, the quartermaster services asked the manufacturers to add a merrowed border to patches to prevent them from deteriorating when garments were washed. To do this, each patch was taken individually after being cut from the strip as it came out of the embroidery machine. The operation was initially carried out manually, then automatically. This procedure had been used by some manufacturers since the nineteen-forties, mostly with civilian patches (State, police, fire fighters, Red Cross, civil defence and so on) and a few military patches.

1966-68 saw the appearance of a subdued variation of each patch designed for wear on combat uniforms. These generally comprise of embroidered black motifs on an olive drab background. 1991 saw the introduction of a "desert" version comprising of brown motifs on a tan background. These were replaced less than ten years later (circa 2003-2004) by patches designed for the new Army Combat Uniform (ACU), the black motifs of which are embroidered onto a grey-green backing. These patches have velcro TM on their reverse to attach to the garments. As for the colour patches retained for the service uniform, they are doubled on the reverse with gray twill that is attached when the merrowed edging is carried out.

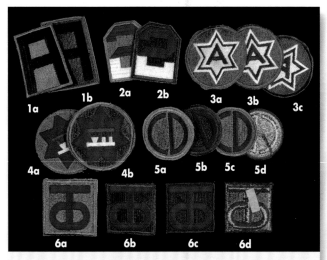

Types of manufacture, 1940-2009

1a *1st Army, manufacture 1940-49 (the cloth patch became red, white and black in 1949) on an olive drab backing.*
1b *Subdued version for the combat uniform 1968-2000. Note the merrowed border and the slightly darker olive drab background.*
2a *2nd Army, manufacture 1940-57, olive drab background.*
2b *Manufacture 1957-70, Army Green 44 background.*
3a *6th Army, manufacture 1940-60 with olive drab background.*
3b *Manufacture 1960-70 with AG44 background.*
3c *Manufacture 1970-2000 with AG44 background and merrowed border.*
4a *VII Army Corps, manufacture 1940-65 with olive drab background.*
4b *Manufacture 1968-92 with olive drab background and merrowed border. There is also a version with an AG44 background with flat or merrowed border.*
5a *85th Infantry Division, manufacture 1940-45 with olive drab background and flat border.*
5b *Manufacture 1968-70 with Army Green 44 background, flat border.*
5c *85th (Training) Division, manufacture 1968-70 with olive drab background and merrowed border.*
5d *Reverse of a nineteen-seventies manufactured patch with olive drab background and merrowed border. Note the small "tail" on the merrowed border stitch, characteristic of patches made in this period.*
6a *90th Infantry Division, manufacture 1940-52 with olive drab background and flat border.*
6b *Manufacture 1959-65 with AG44 background and flat border.*
6c *90th Army Reserve Command, manufacture 1968-96, then 90th Regional Support Command from 1996 to 2003, AG44 background and merrowed border.*
6d *Reverse of previous patch, note the small "tail" retained by a piece of adhesive tape.*
7a *Close up of the flat border typical of patches made between 1940 and 1966. The white filling yarn at the rear is typical of the period and is more or less dense depending on the manufacturer, other base colours can be encountered, see further on.*
7b *Close up of a satin stitched merrowed border, characteristic of manufacture between 1966-2003. Note on the reverse the detail of the synthetic thread, the small "tail" and the piece of tape retaining it.*

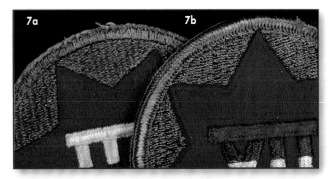

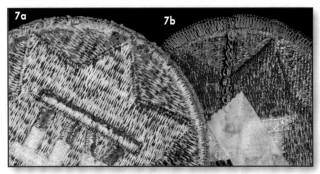

At the rest camp in Ste-Marie (France) late 1944, these Red Cross volunteers, operating a Clubmobile PX truck, stare at a strange and large antique rifle tied above a mudguard. Bobby Bray from Philadelphia, perched on the hood, displays numerous shoulder patches on her field jacket, obviously offered by GI admirers. (Malan Heslop picture, Brigham Young U.)

Above.
An early catalog for patch collectors.

A grouping of patches belonging to a soldier of the 26th Infantry Regiment, 1st Infantry Division. All are theatre made, probably in Germany, circa 1945-46:

A 1st Infantry Division patch with the red cotton thread number known as the "applied" numeral with fine gold bullion edging. The brown twill background, of the type used by the various branches of the Nazi Party, such as the SA or the Organisation Todt, is reinforced with white cloth and glued paper.
This patch was found alone and was no doubt issued to an artillery unit due to its red piping border.

B Distinctive Unit Insignia of the 26th Infantry Regiment, blue thread arrowhead stitches embroidered onto white felt and edged with gold bullion, all of which is placed on brown wool, reinforced on the reverse with strong white twill.

C The same patch, German-made in painted brass with screw back fixation system.

D Combat Infantryman Badge, embroidered with matt silver bullion, also typical of German-made insignia, on light blue felt, all of which is placed on a brown background identical to patch A.

E Overseas Stripes, silver bullion embroidered on the same twill (two bars = 1 year of overseas service).

F Badge made for wear on a civilian jacket lapel, painted on metal with screw back fixation system.

7

A · · · · · · · · · · B · · · · · · · · · · C

D · · · · · · · · · · E

Variations of patches' backs

Above, a few examples of typical backs of WW2 US manufacture patches.
A European Theater of Operations (patch will be described in the following volume). White weave thread on back, the most commonly observed, the whiter the thread, the earlier the manufacture.
B Multi-colored back weave thread.
C European Theatre of Operations, pink back, a rarity.
D & E IX Corps and IIIrd Armored Corps, 'green back' in various hues. This topic will be dealt with in greater depth in the next volume.

A few repros

Below, several examples of current reproductions of WW2 patches, either fully embroidered, or embroidered on felt or wool, seen front and back. All feature synthetic thread. This topic will also be dealt with in greater depth in the next volume.
1 2d Infantry Division (see page 31)
2 36th Infantry Division (see page 49)
3 90th Infantry Division (see page 71)
4 103rd Infantry Division (see page 79)

1 · · · · · · · · · · 2 · · · · · · · · · · 3 · · · · · · · · · · 4

Right.
1942 enlisted man's service coat, for a corporal in the 30th Infantry/3rd Infantry Division. Lepels bear the regimental Distinctive Insignia.
– On the chest: Combat Infantryman Badge and ribbons (Army Good Conduct Medal and European-African-Middle Eastern Campaign Medal)
– Around the left arm: French fourragère in the Croix de Guerre colors
– Lower left sleeve: three Overseas Stripes (one = six months)
– Above the right hand pocket: the blue Distinguished Unit Citation.
(Author's collection)

Below.
1942 enlisted man's service coat for a sergeant in the 77th Field Artillery Battalion (9th Army). Ribbon bar for: Army Good Conduct Medal, American Campaign Medal and European-African-Middle Eastern Campaign Medal (two bronze campaign stars), Sharpshooter badge with Rifle and Field Artillery bars. On the left sleeve bottom, three Overseas service stripes.
(Author's collection)

9

Above.
M-1944 wool field jacket for a Medical Department
soldier assigned to the 75th Infantry Division.
– Right shoulder: 'Combat' Patch for the Alaskan Department
– Right pocket: Honourable Discharge Emblem.
— Above left pocket: ribbon bar for the American Defense Service Medal,
American Campaign, European-African-Middle Eastern Campaign Medal
(three campaign stars),
and Asiatic-Pacific Campaign Medal.
– Lower left sleeve: oblique OD stripe for one year Federal Service and seven
gold overseas service stripes.
(Author's collection)

Left.
M-1943 field jacket for a 28th Division officer. The shirt collar bears
a 1st Lieutenant silver bar and 109th Field Artillery Battalion branch insignia.
(Author's collection)

Right.
M-1944 wool field jacket for a Technician 4th Grade in the 379th Infantry (95th Division):
– 9th Division 'Combat' Patch on right sleeve
– above left pocket: Combat Infantryman Badge (CIB) and ribbon bar for the: Army Good Conduct Medal and European-African-Middle Eastern Campaign Medal
– Marksman' 1921 pattern shooting badge with Rifle bar. Domed collar disks are a typical late war fashion.
(Author's collection)

Below.
Early war private purchase Mackinaw coat for a 87th Infantry Division lieutenant-colonel. Garment is fully reversible, with a wool side and a poplin side. Rank insignia and shoulder patch are fully embroidered and stitched on both sides.
(Author's collection)

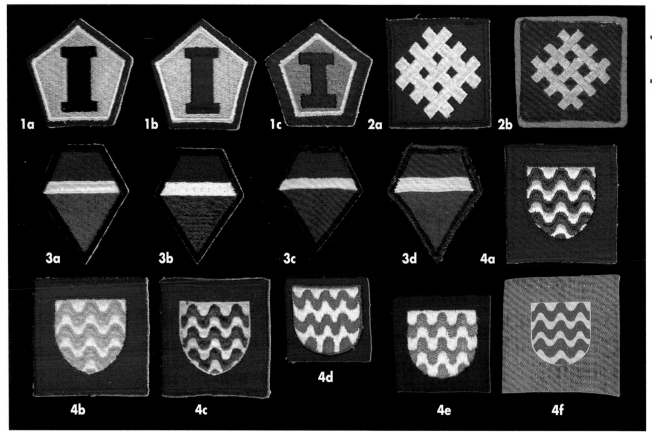

ARMY GROUPS

1 - 1st Army Group

AC: London 19 October 1943. Became the Twelfth Army Group on 14 July 1944. Remained on paper for the command elements of phantom units during Operation Fortitude.
A: 28 March 1944.
S: Roman numeral 1 with national colours.
M: To administer and train troops for Operation Overlord and to prepare an administrative plan for the continent in the event of German surrender before the landings. These two actions were jointly carried out with the British 21st Corps and under SHAEF authority.
C: 30, only for the Communication Platoon/72nd Public Service Bn. for Operation Fortitude.

1a *Standard type (described as having a blue background which is, in fact, light gray blue).*
1b *Standard type with light blue background.*
1c *Patch for artillery units allocated to army groups (red is the traditional arm of service colour).*

2 - 6th Army Group

AC: Bastia (Corsica), 1 August 1944. Inactivated in July 1945.
A: 23 October 1944.

S: six interlaced bars for the numeric designation.
M: operational control of units planned for the landings in Provence (7th US Army, 1st French Army, 1st Allied Airborne Task Force and 1st Special Service Force).
C: 25 (advanced Phalsbourg HQ personnel on 14 December 1944) - 26 - 34 - 37.

2a *Standard patch, solid bars.*
2b *British made patch, embroidered on red felt and sewn on a piece of wool shirt material.*

3 - 12th Army Group

AC: In France, 14 July 1944, with personnel of the General Staff of the First Army Group. Inactivated on 31 July 1945.
A: 29 July 1944.
S: Arrowhead stitching in national colours. The five sides of the pentagon (5) + the red trapezoid (4) + the blue isosceles triangle (3) = 12 for the numeric designation.
M: Supervised the activities of the 1st and 3rd Armies under the operational control of the British 21st Army Group. On 5 September 1944, the 9th Army was added, followed by the 15th Army in January 1945. This was the biggest American formation with 39 infantry divisions and 15 armored divisions.
C: 25 - 26 - 30 - 34.

3a *Standard model with thin edging on the white bar.*
3b *Variation without edging. Note on patch 3a the horizontal embroidery on the red and blue areas, but which is vertical on the white bar, whereas the opposite applies on patch 3b. This is due to a different machine setting and*

does not necessarily indicate a different manufacturer. This rule applies to many other patches in this publication.
3c British made, embroidered on blue wool.
3d European made in several pieces of cloth, the reverse is strengthened with black twill.

4 - 15th Army Group

AC: In Algiers 10 July 1943. Re-designated Headquarters Allied Central Mediterranean Force in January 1944, then Headquarters Allied Armies in Italy in March 1944, then returning to its original designation in December 1944. Inactivated on 15 July 1945, its personnel were transferred to HQ United States Forces in Austria.
A: 5 May 1944, authorized for wear by American personnel by the British General Alexander on 29 January 1945.

ARMIES

The main role of armies, large units that more often existed only on paper before the war, was to oversee army corps that were attached to them. The army was responsible for logistics such as supplies, fuel, ammunition and rations etc. for the army corps with the latter then being able to concentrate on training troops, maneuvers in the field and combat itself.

5 - 1st Army

AC: 10 August 1918 at La Ferté-sous-Jouarre (France). Inactivated on 20 April 1919 at Marseilles (France). Re-activated on 11 September 1933 and based at Fort Jay (Governor's Island/New York).
A: 18 November 1918 by the American Expeditionary Force, confirmed in October 1933.
S: letter A for Army and first letter of the alphabet.
C: 25 - 26 - 30 - 32 - 34.

S: mediterranean waves, national colours common to the British and Americans.
M: grouped together the British 8th Army and American 7th Army, the latter made way for the 5th Army after Sicily.
C: 29 - 31 - 35 - 36.

Except for the British made variations (with black borders, embroidered or printed), one can identify two American made variations:
4a Standard pattern with dark blue waves and a thin red border around the central shield.
4b Variation, light blue waves.
4c Variation, white border around the shield.
4d British made with red felt. Note the difference in the design of the waves.
4e Variation, black twill glued to the reverse.
4f Canadian made, printed on twill. We again see here the American waves in a slightly different design.

5a American made in 1930-40, large size (75 x 90 mm), embroidered on wool.
On the following patches, the central colours correspond to the arms and services. This system was abandoned circa 1942-43, and the patches were sold in the PX stores until the stock ran out. This type of patch exists in two main types of manufacture: embroidered on wool and totally embroidered, the latter being more typical of WW2.
5b Artillery.
5c Engineers, probably theatre or tailor made.
5d Military police.
5e Standard WW2 patch.
5f Variation, with edging around the A.
5g A more olive drab base colour, perhaps for the summer uniform.
5h Approximately 1930-42, for the summer uniform.
5i British made, WW2, printed on thick twill with a black back.
5j Late war patch, white and red being the colours of Army flags.
This more visible patch was more likely worn by color or honor guards. It should not be confused with the new 1950s insignia (black A over a half white-half red background).

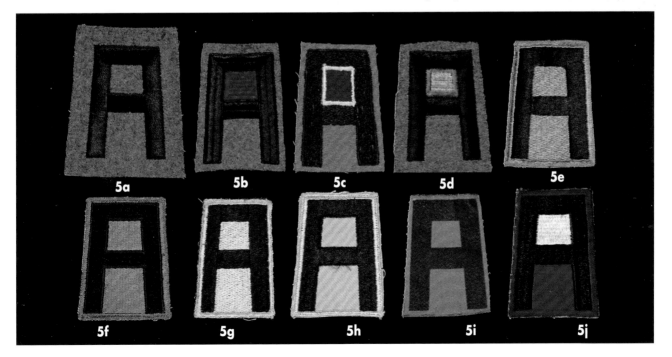

1st Army (continued)

5k *Infantry.*
5l *Artillery, on uniform serge cloth.*
5m *Engineers, identical type to 5e, the colours are hand embroidered.*
5n *Engineers, theatre made on shirt cloth. 5o Signals.*
5o *Transmissions.*
5p *Quartermaster.*
5q *Military police.*
5r *Medical services.*
5s *Chemical warfare.*

6 - 2nd Army

AC: 20 September 1918 at Toul (France). Inactivated on 15 April 1919. Reactivated 9 August 1922 and activated 1 October 1933 in Chicago (Illinois), staff at Memphis (Tennessee) when war was declared.

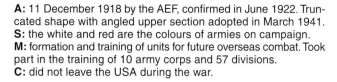

A: 11 December 1918 by the AEF, confirmed in June 1922. Truncated shape with angled upper section adopted in March 1941.
S: the white and red are the colours of armies on campaign.
M: formation and training of units for future overseas combat. Took part in the training of 10 army corps and 57 divisions.
C: did not leave the USA during the war.

6a *Manufacture 1930-40, embroidered on wool, rectangular.*
6b *Embroidered patch, 1940/WW2. Note the embroidery of the base of the rectangle, this type of manufacture was also American.*
6c *Standard WW2 type, three-strip embroidery of number 2.*
6d *Standard patch enhanced with silver bullion and red thread, this type of enhancement was not only carried out by US tailors, but also in theatres of operations.*
6e *1935-40 for the summer uniform, light olive drab twill.*
6f *Variation, with olive drab border.*

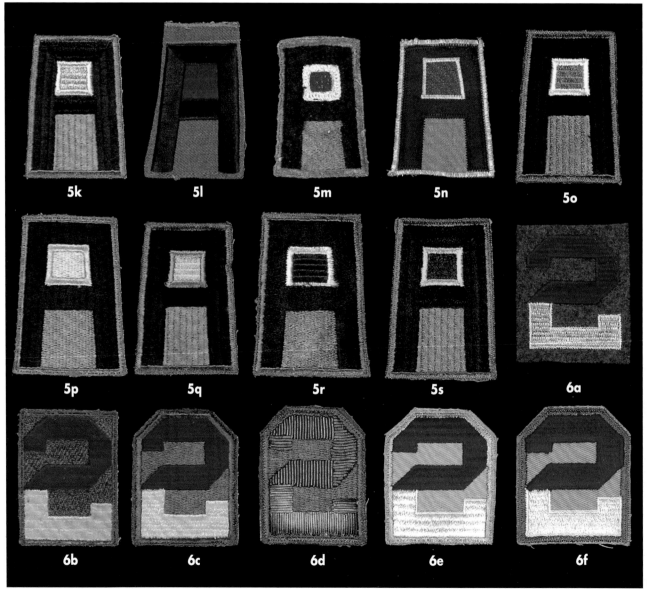

5k   5l   5m   5n   5o

5p   5q   5r   5s   6a

6b   6c   6d   6e   6f

1st Army

2nd Army

14

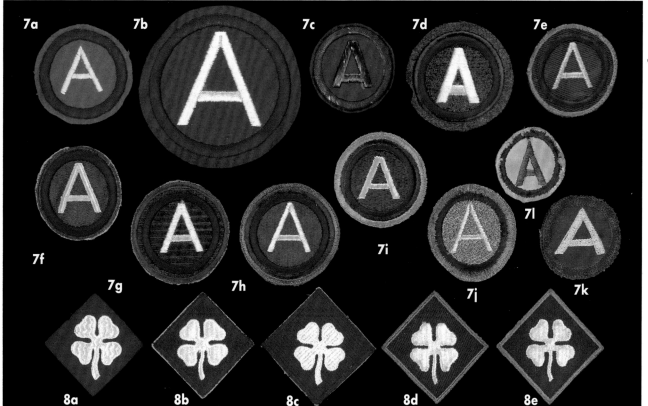

7 - 3rd Army

AC: 7 to 15 November 1918 at Ligny en Barrois (France) under the name of 3rd Army/Army of Occupation. Inactivated on 2 July 1919 becoming American Forces in Germany. Returned to the United States in June 1922. Re activated on 9 August 1932 at Fort Sam Houston (Texas).
A: 20 December 1918 by the AEF, confirmed in 1932.
S: Letters A and O for Army of Occupation along with national colours.
C: 25 - 26 - 30 - 32 - 34.

7a *1930-40, embroidered on blue felt (diameter 61 mm).*
7b *Variation, large size, probably intended for sport garments.*
7c *European made WW2, embroidered with red cotton and silver bullion on felt.*
7d *1930-40, embroidered on wool.*
7e *1940/WW2, embroidered on twill with olive drab border.*
7f *Standard manufacture (diameter 58 mm).*
7g *Variation, identified as being German made by some American authors.*
7h *Variation, fully embroidered with olive drab border.*
7i *Variation, light olive drab border, British made according to some American authors.*
7j *Probably French made, very thin base cloth and very light embroidery.*
7k *European manufacture, chain stitch embroidery on thin blue cloth.*
7l *European made, inverted colours, on white twill.*

8 - 4th Army

AC: activated on 9 August 1932 in Omaha (Nebraska), on active service upon declaration of war, HQ at Presidio de San Francisco (California).
A: authorized on 8 September 1926, approved on 26 January 1927, confirmed in August 1932.

S: the flour-leaf clover for the numeric designation and as a lucky symbol. Designed by Arthur E. Dubois of the Heraldry Section of the Office of the Quartermaster General.
M: Training for troops stationed west of the Mississippi. Between January 1944 and the end of the war, the 4th Army ensured the administration and training of more than 282,000 men.
C: Remained in the USA throughout the war.

8a *Standard manufacture, on red felt, 1930-40.*
A circular-shaped type was in existence during the nineteen-thirties. 1930.
8b *Standard manufacture, WW2*
8c *Variation, different embroidery pattern. Some authors identify this type as being German made.*
8d *Standard manufacture, the olive drab border disappeared circa 1942-43.*
8e *Variation.*

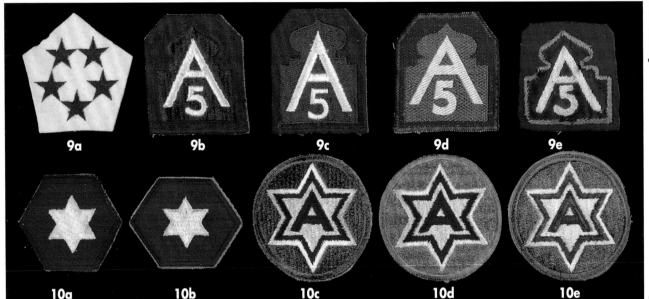

9a   9b   9c   9d   9e

10a   10b   10c   10d   10e

9 - 5th Army

AC: activated 1 December 1942. Organized on 5 January 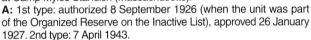 1943 at Oujda (Morocco). Inactivated on 2 October 1945 at Camp Myles Standish (Massachusetts).

A: 1st type: authorized 8 September 1926 (when the unit was part of the Organized Reserve on the Inactive List), approved 26 January 1927. 2nd type: 7 April 1943.

S: 1st type, five stars for the numeric designation, with two traditional colours. Designed by Arthur E. Dubois.
2nd type, number 5, the mosque door symbolizes the place of activation, all of which is accompanied by national colours. Designed by Colonel Maurice R. Barker.

C: 24 - 29 - 31 - 33 - 35.

9a *1st type (1926-43), on white felt.*
9b *2nd type, standard American manufacture, mosque door with thin red border.*
9c *Variation, thin blue border.*
9d *Woven patch, identified as being of Italian manufacture by American authors.*
9e *Theatre made, North Africa or Italy, in felt and silk.*

10 - 6th Army

AC: activated on 22 January 1943 and organized 25 January at Fort Sam Houston (Texas). Inactivated 26 January 1946 in Kyoto (Japan).

A: 1st type authorized 8 September 1926 when the unit was assigned to the Organized Reserve on the Inactive List. Approved 26 January 1927. 2nd type: 10 January 1945.

S: 1st type: six-point star, traditional colours, designed by Arthur E. Dubois. 2nd type: six-point star, traditional colours and A for Army. The unit's nickname was Alamo Force after the area where it was activated.

C: 3 - 13 - 14 - 15.

10a *1st type, 1927-45.*
10b *Variation, vertical embroidery (the first type existed with the red number six in the centre of the star).*
10 c, d & e *2nd type, 1945/46, standard American manufacture.*

11 - 7th Army

AC: activated on 25 February 1943 by re-designating the 1st Armored Corps and organized 10 July 1943 off the coast of Sicily. Inactivated on 31 March 1946.

A: 23 June 1943.

S: the initial A for Army comprises of seven steps for the numeric designation. Colours of the three main arms (blue for infantry, red for artillery and yellow for cavalry).

C: 25 - 26 - 34 - 35 - 36 - 37.

11a *Standard WW2 manufacture.*
11b *Variation, different embroidery, identified by some American authors as being German made, the yellow border might indicate a cavalry unit.*
11c *WW2 European manufacture, chain stitch embroidery on felt.*
11d *Woven European manufacture (or American?) 1945, black felt backing.*
11e *European made, 1945, probably German given the type of bullion used, thick white strengthening twill on the reverse.*
11f *Variation above, embellished with a metallic silk along the border, glued paper on the reverse.*
11g *Probably British made, printed on twill.*
11h-i- *Non-regulation shoulder scrolls worn by veterans of the European campaigns when they returned to the United States in 1945/46.*

Note. It is difficult to accurately date European made variations. Indeed, the unit remained in Germany until 1946 then, after returning to the United States, was sent back to Germany in 1950 where it remained until the bulk of American forces left this country between 1995-2000. It is possible, therefore, that patches 11e and 11f date from the 1950s.

12 - 8th Army

AC: activated 2 June 1944 and organized on 10 June 1944 in Memphis (Tennessee).

A: 10 May 1944.

S: octagon for the numeric designation in traditional colours.

C: 13-14-15.

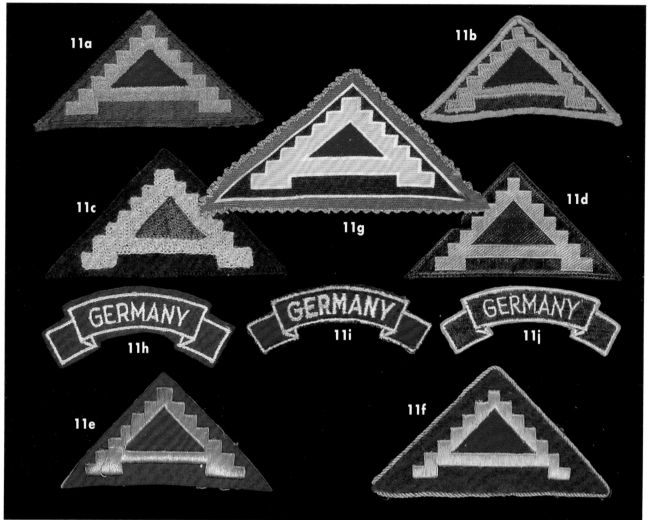

11a

11b

11c

11g

11d

11h GERMANY

11i GERMANY

11j GERMANY

11e

11f

12a Standard WW2 manufacture.
12b Variation, enhanced with gilt metallic thread, reinforcing paper glued to the reverse.
12c Standard manufacture with olive drab border normally more in use at the time of the patch's creation. One cannot dismiss the hypothesis that this was manufactured for collectors. Olive drab bordered patches are very sought after in the United States and often reach very high prices.
12d Theatre made manufacture, WW2, or tailor made. Bullion embroidery on red felt, reinforcing paper glued to the reverse.
12e Variation, with silver metallic thread border, thin white silk on the reverse.

It is also very difficult to accurately date the theatre made versions of this patch; the 8th Army remained as an occupying force in Japan, then went to the Korean War (1950-53).

Publisher's note

The publisher would like to highlight that the patches seen here are just a small part of the author's huge collection. This led, therefore, to a difficult choice in order to present only standard manufactures and the most typical variations.

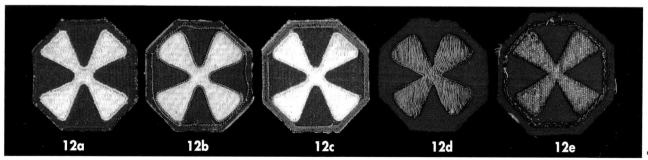

12a

12b

12c

12d

12e

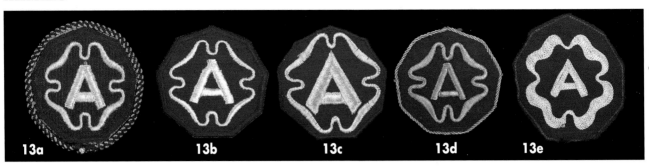

13a | 13b | 13c | 13d | 13e

13 - 9th Army

AC: activated on 15 April 1944 at Fort Sam Houston (Texas), under the name of 8th Army. Re-designated 9th Army on 22 May 1944 in order to avoid any confusion with the British 8th Army. Inactivated on 10 October 1945 at Fort Bragg (North Carolina).
A: 21 September 1944.
S: nonagon representing the numeric designation, letter A for Army. The white quatrefoil shaped border evokes the origin of the unit's officers who came from the 4th Army. All of this is associated with traditional colours.
C: 26 - 32 - 34.

13a *Standard WW2 manufacture. The patch is embellished with garrison cap piping in the traditional colours of the engineers. Such embellishment was fairly widespread.*
13b *Variation, type of embroidery identified in the USA as being of German origin.*
13c *Theatre made, perhaps British, on red felt with thin black reinforcing twill on the reverse.*
13d *German made, 1945, matt silver bullion, matt silver metallic silk along the border, paper glued to the reverse.*
13e *European made, embroidered with chain stitching on thin red twill, red reinforcing cloth on the reverse.*

14 - 10th Army

AC: activated on 20 June 1944 at Fort Sam Houston (Texas). Inactivated on 15 October 1945 in Okinawa.
A: 29 August 1944.
S: two inverted triangles forming the Roman numeral 10 with two traditional colours.
C: 19.

14a *Standard manufacture, WW2.*
14b *Variation, small-size white triangles.*
14c *Theatre made or tailor made, embroidered with thick silk thread, white triangles on felt, all on olive drab wool.*
14d *Non-regulation shoulder scroll.*

15 - 15th Army

AC: activated 21 August 1944 at Fort Sam Houston (Texas). Inactivated 31 January 1946 in Bad Neuheim (Germany).
A: 23 October 1944.
S: the crossed-over traditional colours form the Roman numeral ten along with the five sides of the pentagon.
C: 34.

15a & b *Standard manufacture. There is a patch without an olive drab border which is, for a change, rarer.*

Glossary

● **Activate:** to put into existence by an official Army order a unit which has been previously constituted and designated by name or number, so that it can be organized.
● **Assign:** change in a unit's status, placed on a long-term basis to one of the army components (Active, Reserve, National Guard).
● **Constitute:** creation of a unit on paper. Decided by the Secretary for War and approved by Congress, which explains the possible process of deactivation (see further on).
● **Demobilize:** placing a unit on a peacetime footing or mothballed.
● **Designate:** attribution of title to a unit, generally consisting of a name or number.
● **Inactivate:** placing a unit on a non-operational footing, without personnel or equipment. Such units can therefore be reactivated without Congress approval, as they have not officially ceased to exist.
● **Disband:** removing a unit from the official list, it can only be re-activated with Congress approval.
● **Organize:** to put a unit into physical existence by assigning personnel and equipment.
● **Reconstitute:** reintegration into the official army list a unit previously inactivated. This unit can take back its original name or number, or receive new ones.
● **Redesignate:** change of name, number or both with a previously activated unit.
● **Reorganize:** changing the structure of a unit in agreement with new organizational tables, or changing the unit type, for example going from a horse equipped cavalry unit to a mechanized unit, or transforming an anti-aircraft or tank destroyer unit into an infantry or military police unit etc.

14d OKINAWA | 14a | 14b | 14c | 15a | 15b

CHRONOLOGY OF CAMPAIGNS

Three major theatres of operations were defined by the American forces general staff during the course of the Second World War. Service in each of these areas was the subject of the award of a commemorative medal.

● **American Theater:** encompassing North America, excluding Alaska, South America and the western part of the Atlantic Ocean and an eastern quarter of the Pacific. Three campaigns were retained for this theatre of operations, only for air forces.

● **Asiatic-Pacific Theater:** Encompassing the entire Pacific Ocean and a large part of Asia (including Alaska and Hawaii). 21 recognized campaigns.

● **European-African-Middle Eastern Theater:** encompassing all of Europe (including Greenland) Africa and the Middle-East, the eastern half of the Atlantic Ocean, the Mediterranean and the eastern half of the Indian Ocean. 17 recognized campaigns.

La participation à une campagne autorise l'ajout d'une étoile sur le ruban de la médaille correspondante.

Participation in a campaign authorized the addition of a star on the ribbon of the corresponding medal. Campaigns are identified by one or several numbers in each unit's paragraph. The presence of an arrowhead (▲) signifies that the unit took part in the first wave of landings or an airborne operation. This particularity was authorized on 23 December 1944.

Note: campaigns 1 and 22 only concern the USAAF.

Campaigns of the Pacific theatre of operations

1. *Aerial offensive against Japan: 12 April 1942 - 12 September 1943.*
2. *Aleutian Islands: 3 June 1942 - 24 August 1943.*
3. *Bismarck Island archipelago: 15 December 1943 - 27 November 1944.*
4. *Burma 1942: 7 December 1941 - 26 May 1942.*
5. *Central Burma: 29 January to 15 July 1945.*
6. *Central Pacific: 7 December 1941 - 6 December 1943.*
7. *China, defensive phase: 4 July 1942 - 4 May 1945.*
8. *China, phase: 5 May to 2 September 1945.*
9. *South Pacific: 1 January to 22 July 1942.*
10. *Central Pacific: 31 January to 14 July 1944.*
11. *Guadalcanal: 7 August 1942 - 21 February 1943.*
12. *India - Burma: 2 April 1942 - 28 January 1943.*
13. *Leyte (Philippines): 17 October 1944 - 1 July 1945.*
14. *Luzon (Philippines): 15 December 1944 - 4 July 1945.*
15. *New Guinea: 24 January 1943 - 31 December 1944.*
16. *Salomon Islands - North: 22 February 1943 - 21 November 1944.*
17. *Papua: 23 July 1942 - 23 January 1943.*
18. *Philippines archipelago: 7 December 1941 - 10 May 1942.*
19. *Ryukyu Islands: 26 March to 2 July 1945.*
20. *Philippines archipelago - South: 27 February to 4 July 1945.*
21. *Western Pacific: 15 June 1944 - 2 September 1945.*

Campaigns of the European-African-Middle Eastern theatre of operations

22. *Aerial offensive - Europe: 4 July 1942 - 5 June 1944.*
23. *Algeria - French Morocco: 8 to 11 November 1942.*
24. *Anzio (Italy): 22 January to 24 May 1944.*
25. *Ardennes-Alsace: 16 December 1944 - 25 January 1945.*
26. *Central Europe: 22 March to 11 May 1945.*
27. *Egypt - Libya: 11 June 1942 - 12 February 1943.*
28. *Ground combat - Europe-Africa-Middle East (reserved for the USAAF): 11 May 1942 - 8 May 1945.*
29. *Naples-Foggia (Italy): 9 September 1943 - 21 January 1944.*
30. *Normandy: 6 June - 24 July 1944.*
31. *Northern Apennines (Italy): 10 September 1944 - 4 April 1945.*
32. *Northern France: 25 July - 14 September 1944.*
33. *Po Valley (Italy): 5 April to 8 May 1945.*
34. *Rhineland: 15 September 1944 - 21 March 1945.*
35. *Rome-Arno (Italy): 22 January to 9 September 1944.*
36. *Sicily: 9 July to 17 August 1943.*
37. *Southern France: 15 August to 14 September 1944.*
38. *Tunisia: 17 November 1942 - 13 May 1943.*

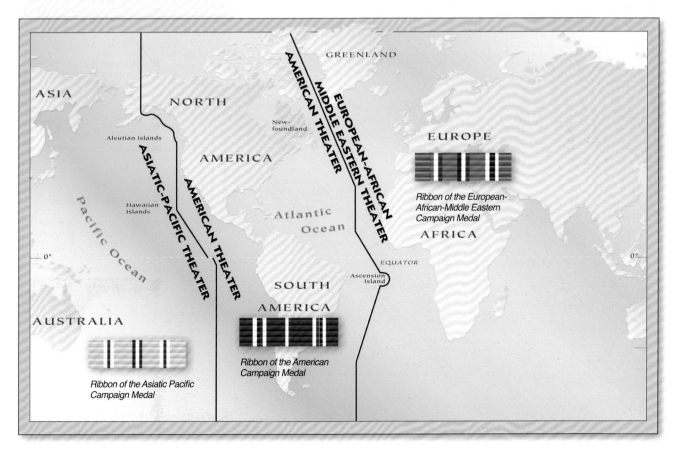

Ribbon of the European-African-Middle Eastern Campaign Medal

Ribbon of the American Campaign Medal

Ribbon of the Asiatic Pacific Campaign Medal

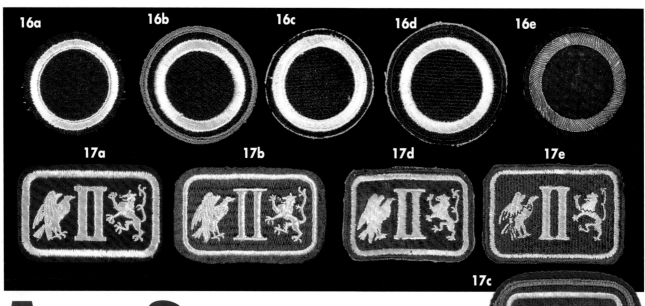

ARMY CORPS

At the beginning of the war, the United States were divided into 9 Corps Areas. Under the impulse of General MacArthur, the Chief of Staff (1930-35), four Field Armies were organized, on paper, comprising of two (or more) army corps. The army corps commanders were responsible for all establishments and units in their jurisdiction. The role of army corps was to cover tactical, administrative and supply aspects for these forces. These nine corps were numbered I to IX in Roman numerals in order to avoid any confusion with armies and divisions. Shortly before the Second World War, nine new corps overlapped geographically with the other corps and were numbered by adding ten units to the active corps numbers to which they were associated.

During the war, the army corps staffs were taken for overseas service and their USA based tasks were placed in the hands of Service Commands. Each overseas army corps comprised of organic corps troop**s**: aerial observation, artillery, military police, medical services, signals, engineers, intelligence, quartermaster, equipment, transport etc.

It was decided, in 1943, to transfer many corps troops to the armies. The army corps only retained, on average, a staff, a military police platoon, a signals battalion, two or three artillery battalions and an artillery observation battalion.

16 - I Corps

AC: activated between 15 and 20 January 1918 in Neufchâteau (France). Inactivated 25 March 1919. Reactivated 15 August 1927 under the name of XX Corps. Re-designated I Corps on 13 October 1927. Inactivated in Japan 28 March 1950.

A: 3 December 1918 by the AEF, then changed on 17 June 1922, on the request of the Secretary for War, without any known explanation. Confirmed in November 1940.
S: initially a white circle with blue background, the army corps' colours, then with a black background for unknown reasons. This design is taken from that of the Union Army's I Army Corps (1800-05).
C: 9 - 14 - 15 - 17.

16a *Standard manufacture 1930-40, embroidered on black wool with white gauze on the reverse.*
16b *Standard manufacture 1938-42, green border and green weave thread on reverse.*

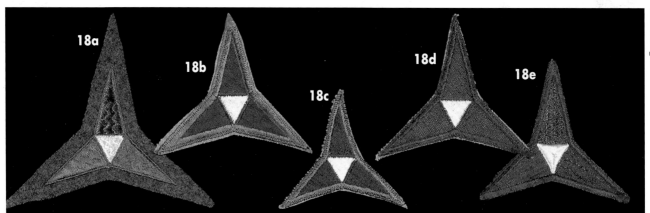

16c *Standard manufacture, WW2.*
16d *Variation, white border.*
16e *Theatre made or American tailor made, diameter 57 mm, silver bullion border.*

17 - II Corps

AC: activated 24 February 1918 at Montreuil (France). Inactivated 1 February 1919 in Le Mans (France). Reactivated 15 August 1927 as the XXI Army Corps. Re-designated II Corps on 13 October 1927. Inactivated 10 October 1945 in Austria.
A: 13 January 1919 by the AEF, confirmed in August 1940.
S: traditional colours, Roman numeral two. The British lion and American eagle are a reminder of joint service during the Great War.
C: 23 - 29 - 31 - 33 - 35 - 36 - 38.

17a *Standard manufacture 1930-40, embroidered on blue wool, thin black reinforcing twill on the reverse.*
17b *Variation, embroidered on olive green wool.*
17c *Standard manufacture 1938-42, green border, embellished with garrison cap artillery piping.*
17d *Standard manufacture, WW2 (68 x 48 mm).*
17e *German made, eagle and lion variations with detailing in blue.*

18 - III Corps

AC: activated 16 May 1918 in Mussy-sur-Seine (France). Inactivated 9 August 1919 at Camp Sherman (Ohio). Reactivated 15 August 1927 under the name of XXII Corps. Re-designated III Corps 13 October 1927. Inactivated 10 October 1946 at Camp Polk (Louisiana).
A: 3 December 1918 by the AEF, confirmed in December 1940. Type with olive drab border authorized in March 1943.
S: the three spikes of a caltrop as well as a white triangle for the numeric designation, army corps colours. Nickname: 'Century Corps.
C: 25 - 26 - 32 - 34.

18a *Standard manufacture 1930-40, large size.*
18b *Standard manufacture, 1938-42, olive drab border, thin blue border to white triangle.*
18c *Variation, small size.*
18d *Standard WW2 manufacture, thin blue border around the white triangle.*
18e *Variation, 73 x 58 mm, 'German' type embroidery.*

19 - IV Corps

AC: activated 20 June 1918 in Neufchâteau (France). Inactivated 11 May 1919 in Germany. Assigned 29 July 1921 to the Organized Reserve. Reactivated 10 October 1939 at Fort Benning (Georgia). Inactivated 13 October 1945 at Camp Kilmer (New Jersey).
A: 28 December 1918 by the AEF, confirmed in October 1939. Type with olive drab border authorized in October 1942.
S: three quarters of a circle for the numerical designation, traditional colours.
C: 31 - 33 - 35.

19a *Standard manufacture 1930-40 on olive drab wool. The embroidery is very similar to that identified as being German by some authors, something that is doubtful for a pre-war patch!*
19b *Standard WW2 manufacture, without edging to the interior triangles, olive drab border.*
19c *Variation, olive drab border.*
19d *Variation, blurred border to inside triangles.*
19e *Italian made, according to numerous American authors, with design negative on the reverse and topstitched olive drab border.*

20 - V Corps

AC: activated between 7 and 12 July 1918 in Remirecourt (France). Inactivated 2 May 1919 at Camp Funston (Kansas). Assigned 29 July 1921 to the Organized Reserve, inactivated 15 November 1924. Reactivated on 20 October 1940 at Camp Beauregard (Louisiana).
A: 3 December 1918 by the AEF, confirmed in October 1940.
S: the pentagon and the five triangles for the numeric designation, with traditional colours. The pentagon is also a reminder of the 5th Corps emblem used during the Spanish-American War of 1898.
C: 25 - 26 - 30 - 32 - 34.

20a *Standard manufacture 1930-40, embroidered on thin olive drab wool, thin black reinforcing twill on the reverse. There is also a summer version embroidered on khaki twill.*
20b *Standard WW2 manufacture.*
20c *Variation with double white border.*
20d *Standard manufacture, olive drab border.*
20e *Non-regulation red border for the artillery. According to some American authors, this variation is German made.*
There also exists a white 'Germany' tab on a blue background, worn above the patch by veterans upon their return to the United States.

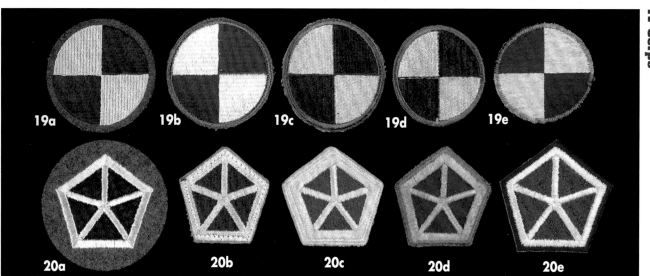

21 - VI Corps

AC: activated between 23 July and 1 August 1918 in Neufchâteau (France). Inactivated in May 1919 at Camp Devens (Massachusetts).

Assigned 29 July 1921 to the Organized Reserve, left the Organized Reserve on 1 October 1933. Reactivated 1 August 1940 at Fort Sheridan (Illinois).

Re-designated VI Army Corps 1 January 1941, then VI Corps 19 August 1942. Re-designated Constabulary Forces HQ 1 May 1946 in Germany.

A: 1 January 1919 by the AEF, confirmed in August 1940.
S: the number six associated with the traditional colours.
C: 24 - 25 - 26 - 29 - 34 - 35 - 37.

21a *Standard WW2 manufacture, diameter 55 mm.*
21b *Variation, diameter 57 mm.*
21c *Variation, olive drab border, diameter 60 mm.*
21d *Variation, large number, diameter 63 mm.*
21e *Variation, embroidery in horizontal stripes, olive drab border.*

22 - VII Corps

AC: activated 19 August 1918 in Remiremont (France). Inactivated from 9 to 11 July 1919 at Camp Upton (New York). Assigned 29 June 1921 to the Organized Reserve, left this organization on 18 October 1927. Reactivated 25 November 1940 at Fort McClellan (Alabama). Reorganized 1 January 1941 as VII Army Corps, re-designated VII Corps 19 August 1942. Inactivated 1 March 1946 at the Presidio of San Francisco.

A: 1st type: 19 November 1918 by the AEF, confirmed in November 1940. 2nd type: 18 August 1944. Worn from April 1944 onwards.

S: 1st type: number seven, traditional corps colours.
2nd type: the seven-point star is similar to the 7th Corps emblem used during the Spanish-American War of 1898.
C: 25 - 26 - 30 - 32 - 34.

22a *1st type patch, embroidered on felt.*
22b *Standard manufacture 1st type patch 1940-44, number thinly outlined in white, green back.*
22c *Variation with olive drab border and horizontal embroidery.*
22d *2nd type patch, standard manufacture, 1944-45.*
22e *German manufacture 1945, with gray reinforcing twill on reverse.*
22f *American manufacture, 'German' type embroidery.*
22g *European made, embroidered on red felt, gauze and filling yarn on reverse.*

23 - VIII Corps

AC: activated 26 to 29 November 1918 in Montigny-sur-Aube (France). Inactivated 29 April 1919 in France. Assigned 29 July 1921 to the Organized Reserve.

Reactivated 14 October 1940 at Fort Sam Houston (Texas). Re-designated VIII Army Corps 1 January 1941, then VIII Corps on 19 August 1942. Inactivated 15 December 1945 at Camp Gruber (Oklahoma).

A: 18 December 1918 by the AEF, confirmed in October 1944.
S: hexagon and number eight, in the corps traditional colours.
C: 25 - 26 - 30 - 32 - 34.

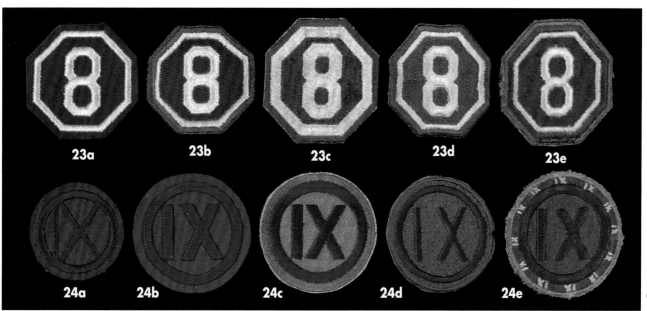

23a *Standard manufacture 1930-40, embroidered on blue felt, thin white gauze on reverse.*
23b *Variation, 1935-42, embroidered on blue twill, thin white gauze on reverse.*
23c *Standard manufacture, number and white border with thin white additional outline.*
23d *Variation, 'German' type embroidery*
23e *Variation, green edge and green back, thin white number and border.*

24 - IX Corps

AC: activated from 25 to 29 November 1918 in Ligny-en-Barrois (France). Inactivated 5 May 1919 in France.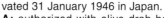
Assigned 29 July 1921 to the Organized Reserve, left the latter on 1 October 1933. Reactivated 24 October 1940 at Fort Lewis (Washington). Re-designated 1 January 1941 as IX Army Corps, then IX Corps once more on 19 August 1942. Inactivated 28 March 1950 in Japan.
A: December 1918 by the AEF, confirmed in June 1922. Confirmed, with smaller Roman numeral, 29 October 1940.
S: Roman numeral 9. The red and blue colours should have been modified to blue and white, the traditional army corps colours, in October 1940.
C: no campaigns to its name.

24a *Standard manufacture 1930-40, embroidered on blue felt; note the Roman numeral merged with the border.*
24b *Standard manufacture 1935-40, red felt sewn on blue felt.*
24c *Standard manufacture, embroidered, WW2.*

24d *Variation, 'German' type embroidery.*
24e *Standard manufacture, 1940-42, olive drab border enhanced with 12 Roman IX numerals as with a clock face, embroidered in orange thread (unknown signification).*

25 - X Corps

AC: constituted 1 May 1942 as the X Army Corps. Activated 15 May 1942 at Camp Sherman (Texas). Redesignated X Corps on 19 August 1942. Inactivated 31 January 1946 in Japan.
A: authorized with olive drab border in May 1942. Approved 19 August 1942.
S: Roman numeral ten for the numeric designation with traditional colours.
C: 13 - 15 - 20.

25a *Standard manufacture, diameter 63 mm.*
25b *Variation, 1938-42, olive drab border, diameter 66 mm.*
25c *Variation, note the absence of horizontal bars to the Roman numeral, diameter 67 mm.*
25d *Theatre made (Japan?) or tailor made, blue felt backing, silver bullion embroidery, on olive drab wool, thin black reinforcing twill glued to reverse diameter 63 mm.*
25e *Variation, worn patch, thin white silk to reverse, also probably Japanese made, diameter 66 mm.*

Note: there is also a model without edging.

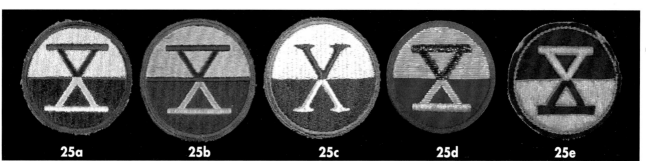

ARMY CORPS

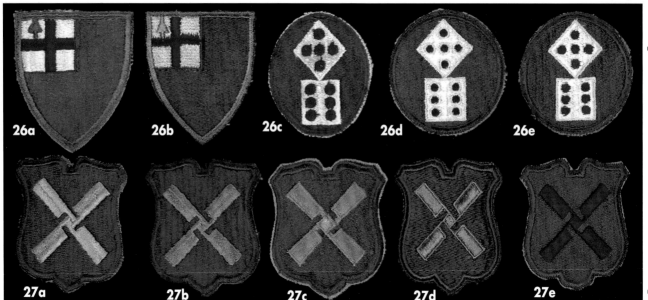

26a 26b 26c 26d 26e

27a 27b 27c 27d 27e

26 - XI Corps

AC: constituted July 1921 in the Organized Reserve on the Inactive List. Re-designated XI Army Corps on 25 April 1942. Activated on 15 June 1942 in Chicago (Illinois). Re-designated XI Corps 19 August 1942. Inactivated 11 March 1945 in Japan.

A: 1st type: 28 June 1922.

2nd type: 3 September 1942. Worn from June 1942 onwards.

S: the 1st type was based on the Bunker Hill flag (1775) and alludes to the unit's garrisons.

2nd type: design in the national colours, the dice for the numeric designation. This combination is that of a famous game and signified that the XI Corps was always the winner. The dice also symbolize luck, always a factor in any military endeavour.

C: 13 - 14 - 15.

26a *Standard manufacture of the 1st type, 1935-43. Dark green pine tree, red cross with thin border.*
26b *Variation, 'German' type embroidery, no outline around the cross. There is a variation without an olive drab border that is rarer.*
26c *Standard manufacture of the 2nd type, WW2, dice with large numbers.*
26d *Variation, small numbers with thin borders.*
26e *Variation, large numbers without border.*

27 - XII Corps

AC: constituted 1 October 1933 in the Organized Reserve as XII Corps. Organized 24 January 1934 in New York. Re-designated XII Army Corps 1 January 1941, then once more on 19 August under the name of XII Corps. Activated on 29 August 1942 and reorganized in Columbia (South Carolina). Inactivated 15 December 1945 in Germany.

A: 26 October 1933.

S: the orange and blue colours come from the House of Nassau coat of arms (Holland), the former owner of the land where the unit was raised. The windmill vanes are taken from the coat of arms of New Amsterdam (the former name of New York before the War of Independence).

C: 25 - 26 - 32 - 34.

27a *Standard WW2 manufacture, light orange vanes.*
27b *Variation, dark orange vanes.*
27c *Variation, blue double border, vanes with thin borders.*
27d *Variation, thin light orange vanes with borders.*
27e *Variation, 'German' type embroidery, red vanes without borders.*

28 - XIII Corps

AC: constituted 1 October 1933 in the Organized Reserve as the XIII Corps. Re-designated 1 January 1941 as XII Army Corps, then once more on 19 August 1942 when it took the name of XIII Corps. Activated and reorganized on 7 December 1942 in Providence (Rhode Island). Inactivated 25 September 1945 at Camp Cooke (California).

A: 7 June 1933, when the unit only existed on paper.

S: the red triangle represents the fact that the first white settlers in the unit's recruitment region were of British origin (Maryland, Pennsylvania and Virginia). The four-leaf clover is the symbol of luck and also forms a Roman ten numeral, joined here with the three sides of the triangle as a numeric designation.

C: 26 - 34.

28a *Standard WW2 manufacture, clover leaf stalk to the left.*
28b *Variation, stalk to the right, manufacture variation.*
28c *Embellished with Corps of Engineers garrison cap piping.*

29 - XIV Corps

AC: constituted 1 October 1933 in the Organized Reserve under the name of XIV Corps. Re-designated 1 January 1941 as XIV Army Corps, then once more on 19 August 1942 under the name of XIV Corps. Activated and reorganized on 19 September 1942 in Brownwood (Texas). Inactivated 31 December 1945 at Fort Lawton (Washington State).

A: 29 September 1933, the unit only existing on paper.

S: gray base and blue cross taken from the Confederate flag. The cross forms the Roman ten numeral, as well as the four-pointed caltrop (see III Corps), all of which points to the numeric designation.

C: 3 - 11 - 14 - 16.

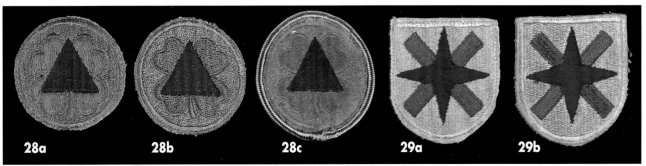

28a · 28b · 28c · 29a · 29b

29a *Standard WW2 manufacture, detailed red star.*
29b *Variation, flat red star.*

30- XV Corps

AC: constituted 1 October 1933 in the Organized Reserve under the name of XV Corps. Re-designated 1 January 1941 as XV Army Corps, then once more on 19 August 1942 as XV Corps. Activated and reorganized 15 February 1943 at Camp Beauregard (Louisiana). Inactivated 31 March 1946 in Germany.
A: 1st type never approved, as yet there is no proof that it was ever worn. 2nd type: 20 April 1943, worn from February 1943 onwards.
S: 1st type, Roman fifteen numeral with traditional colours. 2nd type, blue cross forming the Roman ten numeral and the white chevron the Roman five numeral, in the traditional army corps colours.
C: 25 - 26 - 30 - 34.

30a *Reproduction of the 1st type patch with olive drab border.*
30b *Standard manufacture, WW2, blue straight bar under left bar, thin borders to the Roman numerals, diameter 63 mm.*
30c *Variation, embroidered three bars of the Roman numeral, diameter 60 mm.*
30d *Variation, flat embroidered Roman numeral with thin border, Roman V numeral with thin border.*
30e *European made on officer's gabardine, olive drab edge.*

31 - XVI Corps

AC: constituted 1 October 1933 in the Organized Reserve under the name of XVI Corps. Re-designated 1 January 1941 as XVI Army Corps, then once more on 19 August 1942 under the name of XVI Corps. Activated and reorganized 10 December

1943 at Fort Riley (Kansas). Inactivated 7 December 1945 at Camp Kilmer (New Jersey).
A: 3 April 1944. Worn from December 1943 onwards.
S: designed by Technical Sergeant Howard M. Sargeant. Sixteen tooth cog in traditional colours. The compass rose symbolizes the aptitude to serve in any part of the world. Nickname: 'Compass Corps'.
C: 26 - 34.

31a *Standard manufacture, WW2.*
31b *Variation, wide compass rose, larger star.*
31c *Variation of 31a.*

Note: there is a rare variation with olive drab border rather than blue.

31a · 31b · 31c

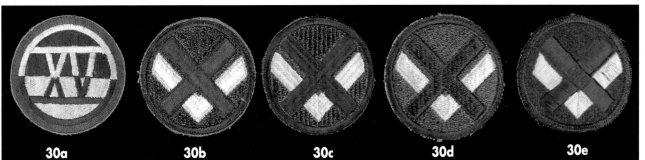

30a · 30b · 30c · 30d · 30e

32 - XVIII Airborne Corps

AC: activated on
14 January 1942 under
the name of II Armored Corps, organized 17 January 1942 at Camp Polk (Louisiana). Re-designated XVIII Corps 9 October 1943, then once more re-designated XVIII Airborne Corps and reorganized 25 August 1944. Inactivated 15 October 1945 at Camp Campbell (Kentucky).

A: 15 February 1944, confirmed for the airborne formation with the patch pivoted by 90 degrees and the addition of an '*Airborne*' tab.

S: Dragon symbolizing cunning, endurance and ferocity. First worn in diamond shape, then square.

C: A - 25 - 26 - 34.

Tasked with logistics and tactics of the Market part of Operation Market Garden (Holland) as well as that of Wesel in support of the Rhine crossing.

32a *Standard manufacture, WW2, diamond shape worn before August 1944, there are a great many variations in the design of the dragon.*
32b *Variation, embroidered on white twill.*
32c *Same as 32a, with the addition of an Airborne tab, the dragon's head seems to prey out of the sky.*
32d *Variation, 1945-50, manufactured in a single piece, embroidered on blue twill.*
32e *Small size for the garrison cap, jacket or service coat. Also exists as an enamelled insignia (patch-type DUI).*
32f *Variation 32d, head facing right, designed to be worn on the right sleeve as a 'Combat patch,' approved on 1 May 1950.*

33 - XIX Corps

AC: constituted on 29 July 1921 in the Organized
Reserve in California. Activated 7 July 1942 as the
III Armored Corps, reorganized and re-designated XIX Corps on 10 October 1943. Inactivated 5 September 1945 in France.

A: 1st type: 6 April 1935.
2nd type: 3 May 1944.
3rd type: 9 March 1949. Worn from late 1944/early 1945, theatre made.

S: 1st type. Bell in Spanish colours, as California had been a territory belonging to the Spanish crown.

2nd type: April 1944 following Eisenhower's request for an Indian tomahawk in the national colours.
3rd type: appeared during the course of the war, French made (the only one worn during the war). Authorized after the war as it was more distinctive than the previous type.

C: 26 - 30 - 32 - 34.

33a *1st type, standard manufacture 1940-42, gold-yellow border.*
33b *2nd type, standard manufacture, thick blue detailing on the tomahawk.*
33c *Variation, white – almost invisible – detailing on the tomahawk.*
33d *3rd Type, French made, dark blue wool, gray inside border, thin white gauze on reverse, diameter 73 mm.*
33e *Standard manufacture of the 3rd type. This late-war patch was mainly worn as a combat patch on the right sleeve by veterans upon their return to the United States, diameter 64 mm.*

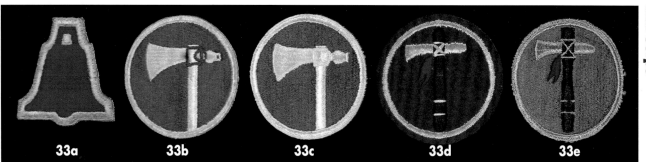

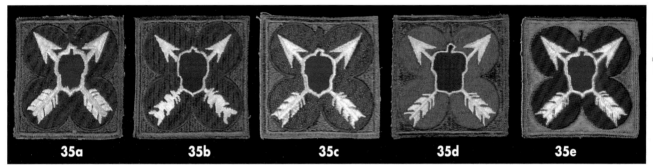

XX CORPS
34a *Standard manufacture, WW2, lemon yellow embroidery, 97 x 83 mm.*
34b *Variation, thinner embroidery, golden yellow, smaller size (94 x 75 mm).*

XXI CORPS
35a *Standard manufacture, WW2.*
35b *Variation, thin border to acorn, without interior separation, arrows with sparse feathers (66 X 70 mm).*
35c *Variation.*
35d *Variation, different shaped acorn.*
35e *Standard manufacture, WW2, embroidered on blue twill, thin white gauze on reverse.*

34 - XX Corps

AC: activated 27 August 1942 under the name of IV Armored Corps, organized 5 September 1942 at Camp Young (California). Reorganized and re-designated XX Corps on 10 October 1943. Inactivated 1 March 1946 in Germany.
A: 4 December 1943.
S: the traditional colours of the infantry, artillery and cavalry. The two pairs of crossed crampons symbolize the unit's determination and tenacity in holding on to terrain, they also form the Roman numeral twenty.
C: 25 - 26 - 30 - 32 - 34.

35 - XXI Corps

AC: activated 2 December 1943, organized 6 December 1943 at Camp Polk (Louisiana). Inactivated 30 September 1945 at Schwabish Gmund in Germany.

A: 3 April 1944.
S: the two crossed arrows represent the fighting spirit, the acorn symbolizes strength and the four-leaf clover luck.
C: 25 - 26 - 34.

36 - XXII Corps

AC: activated 9 January 1944, organized 15 January 1944 at Fort Campbell (Kentucky). Inactivated 20 January 1946 in Germany.
A: 16 April 1944.
S: arrowhead symbolizing power and strength, in the traditional colours.
C: 26 - 34.

XXII CORPS
36a *Standard manufacture, WW2, white over blue embroidery (74 x 67 mm).*
36b *Variation, blue over white embroidery.*
36c *Wider variation (70 mm).*

36d *Theatre made, painted on leather, probably for a pilot's flight jacket (artillery observer, etc.), diameter 95 mm.*

ARMY CORPS

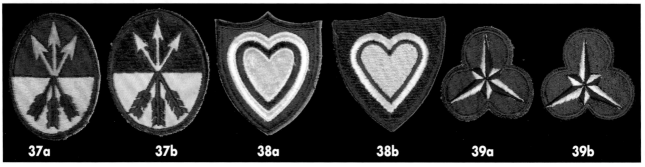

37a   37b   38a   38b   39a   39b

37 - XXIII Corps

AC: activated 9 January 1944, organized 15 January 1944 at Camp Bowie (Texas). Inactivated 10 February 1946 in Wildungen, Germany.
A: 3 April 1944.
S: the three crossed arrows and the two halves of the oval for the numeric designation, in traditional colours. The arrows also symbolize strength.
C: none.

37a *Standard manufacture, WW2.*
37b *Wider variation, embroidered on white twill.*

38 - XXIV Corps

AC: activated 30 March 1944, organized 8 April 1944 at Camp Shafter (Hawaii). Inactivated 25 January 1949 in Korea.
A: 16 August 1944.
S: the heart was the emblem of the Union XXVI Corps during the Civil War, traditional army corps colours.
C: 13 - 19 - 21.

38a *Standard manufacture, WW2.*
38b *Wider variation, 'German' type embroidery.*

39 - XXXVI Corps

AC: activated 1 July 1944, organized 10 July at Fort Riley (Kansas). Inactivated 25 September 1945 at Camp Callan (California). Disbanded 12 July 1950.
A: 17 October 1944.
S: the trefoil and the six points of the stars indicate the numeric designation, along with the three national colours.
M: formed for the invasion of Japan, but the surrender rendered its mission unnecessary and it was deactivated without ever having taken part in combat.
C: none.

39a *Standard manufacture, WW2.*
39b *Variation, off-centre motifs.*
There are also variations with inverted white and red embroidery (manufacturer's error).

During the 29 August 1944 liberation parade on the Paris Champs Elysees, the officials' grandstand is guarded by V Corps MPs, who bear its insignia on their helmets.
(National Archives)

INFANTRY DIVISIONS

21 November 1944, Technician 4th grade Raymond Adams poses after the award the Silver Star for bravery on Saipan. The NCO wears the 27th Infantry Division shoulder patch on the left sleeve of his khaki shirt.
(National Archives)

40 - 1st Infantry Division

AC: activated 24 May 1917, organized under the name of HQ/1st Expeditionary Infantry Division 8 June 1917. Redesignated 1st Division on 6 July 1917. Reorganized and re-designated 1st Infantry Division 1 August 1942.
A: 31 October 1918 by the AEF
S: red number 1 for the numeric designation.
According to legend, the first shoulder patches, consisting of a straight-forward number one, were cut out from the red bands of German caps (Feldmütze).
Nicknames: 'Fighting First - The Red One - The Big Red One.'
Motto: "No Mission too difficult, No sacrifice too great-Duty first!"
C: 23▲ - 25 - 26 - 30s - 32 - 34 - 36 - 38.

40a *1930-40 period patch, embroidered on khaki twill, with oversewn border in the same colour for the summer uniform, thin white gauze on reverse.*
40b *Narrower patch embroidered on wool for the winter uniform.*
40c *Variation.*
40d *Standard manufacture, WW2, fully embroidered, green back.*
40e *Variation, darker background, quite similar to the Army Green 44 of 1955, but made well before this date.*
40f *Identified as 'British made,' 1943-45, very light background, black thread to reverse.*
40g *Theatre made in North Africa or Sicily, 1943, the number is roughly cut out and sewn onto a herringbone twill background.*
40h *British made, 1943-45, embroidered onto olive drab wool, the shield has an olive drab, thin khaki twill to reverse.*
40i *European made 1944-45, number embroidered in red and highlighted with gold bullion, reverse reinforced with thick white twill, gilt silk around the border.*
40j *Woven European made patch, 1944-45, identified as German by several authors.*

Souvenir brochure printed in France in 1945 and handed out to 1st Division soldiers before their return to the States. Several similar booklets are shown in the following pages for other divisions.
(Author's collection)

Codes used in the plate captions

AC: date and place of unit activation
A: official approval date of patch. One should remember that a patch may well have been worn before being authorized.
S: patch symbolism
M: mission
C: Campaigns (see chart on page 19)

41 - 2nd Infantry Division

AC: activated 21 September 1917, organized 26 October in Bourmont (Haute-Marne, France) under the name of 2nd Division. Re-designated 2nd Infantry Division on 1 August 1942.
A: 6 November 1918 by the AEF
S: the national colours of blue, white and red were chosen to mark the Division's baggage and equipment before embarking for France during WW1. An Indian head with war bonnet in these colours was chosen to signify the American origins. During the Great War, a number of shape and colour combinations allowed the identification of the Division's units, down to company/battery level, with thirty such insignia being worn. The only patch authorized was that in the shape of a black shield. Nickname: 'Indian Head.' Motto: "Second to None."
C: 25 - 26 - 30 - 32 - 34.

41a *1930-40 manufacture, Indian head embroidered on a white felt five-pointed star which itself is sewn onto a black felt background.*
41b *1930-40 manufacture, Indian head and white star embroidered on black felt, thin white gauze to reverse.*
41c *1935-40 manufacture, head and star embroidered onto black twill, black border, thin white gauze to reverse.*
41d *WW2 period manufacture, fully embroidered, olive drab border, white back.*
41f *Variation.*
41g *Variation.*
41h *Patch with horizontal type embroidery.*

Combat patches

Examples of two non-regulation 'Combat' patches worn on the left sleeve for the unit in which a soldier saw action before being assigned to another unit. In both cases, the motif (number and Indian head), is inverted to look forward.

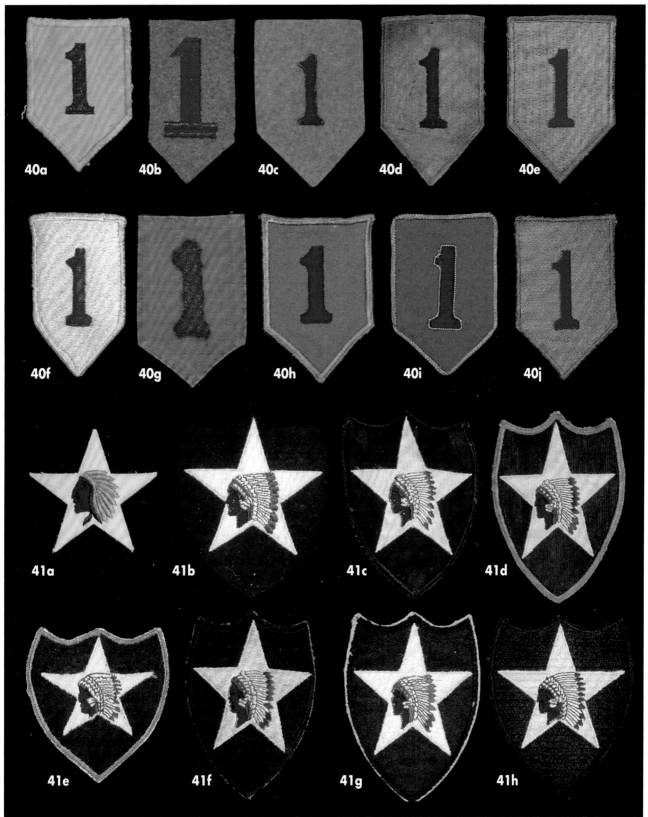

40a 40b 40c 40d 40e

40f 40g 40h 40i 40j

41a 41b 41c 41d

41e 41f 41g 41h

42 - 3rd Infantry Division

AC: activated 12 November 1917 under the name of 3rd Division, organized 21 November at Camp Greene (South Carolina). Re-designated 3rd Infantry Division 1 August 1942.
A: 24 October 1918 by the AEF.
S: the three white stripes symbolize the major operations in which the division took part in 1918. Blue and white are the traditional infantry colours. Nicknames: 'Marne Division,' 'Rock of the Marne.' Motto: "Nous resterons là!"
C: 23▲ - 24▲ - 25 - 26 - 29 - 34 - 35 - 36▲ - 37▲ - 38.

42a *1930-40 manufacture, three white felt stripes sewn onto a blue felt square.*
42b *1930-40 manufacture, three stripes embroidered on blue felt, thin black gauze to reverse.*
42c *Standard WW2 manufacture, fully embroidered with olive drab border, white back. The tab, worn by Anzio veterans, was not authorized.*
42d *Fully embroidered, olive drab border, white back.*
42e *Variation, embroidery known as 'German' type, white back.*
42f *European made, 1943-45, three stripes of white ribbon sewn onto blue wool, thick white gauze to reverse.*
42g *Ditto, Woven in blue and white silk on a wool covered cardboard form, the wool backing having almost disappeared.*
42h *Variation*
42i *Variation, Italian made, 1943, blue stripes printed on white silk, white silk to reverse, thick green border.*
42j *Woven European manufacture, light gray stripes, backed with dark gray twill, green border.*
42k *European made, silver bullion embroidery on blue wool, thick black twill to reverse.*

43 - 4th Infantry Division

AC: activated 19 November 1917 as 4th Division, organized 10 December at Camp Greene (South Carolina). Inactivated 21 September 1921 at Camp Lewis (Washington). Reactivated 1 June 1940 at Fort Benning (Georgia). Reorganized and re-designated 1 August 1942, under the name of 4th Motorized Division. Re-designated and reorganized 4 August 1943 as 4th Infantry Division.
A: 30 October 1918 AEF.
S: four ivy leaves, the symbol of tenacity, for the numeric designation, ivy is also a play on words for the Roman numeral of IV. Nicknames: 'Ivy Division/Famous Fourth'.
C: 25 - 26 - 30▲ - 32 - 34.

Left.
Paris, 26 August 1944. Sergeant Kenneth Averill of the 4th Signal Company receives a warm welcome from the population. The Ivy Division shoulder patch is visible on his shirt sleeve.
(National Archives)

43a *1930-40 manufacture, embroidered on olive drab wool, thick reinforcing white gauze to reverse, leaves with vein detailing.*
43b *1940/42 manufacture, fully embroidered, flat leaves pointing to the corners of the square, white back.*
43c *Variation, background embroidery in stripes, ivy leaf vein detailing, lighter background.*
43d *Variation, embroidery known as 'German,' lighter green leaves, with semi-circular borders and embroidery.*
43e *1940-45 manufacture, same type as 43h, with corners folded to adhere to the regulation WW2 dimensions.*
43f *Known as 'German' type, very light background, curved leaves.*
43g *1935-42 manufacture, embroidered on khaki twill for the summer uniform, angular leaves, tips folded back and stitched.*
43h *1935-40, embroidery known as 'German' type. This large patch (65 x 65 mm) was worn pre-war as such, and during the war more often than not with folded back and stitched corners.*
43i *Variation, green back (68 x 63 mm).*
43j *European made, 1944-45, embroidered in green silk on brown wool, thick black twill to reverse (55 x 55 mm).*
43k *Variation, olive drab 33 colour wool, gold bullion border, thin white gauze to reverse (57 x 57 mm).*
43l *Variation, finer and lighter green thread, embellished with silver bullion, olive drab felt background, thin white gauze to reverse (60 x 60 mm).*
43m *Variation, embroidered on olive drab serge.*
43n *Woven European made patch, reinforced with black felt to reverse (50 x 50 mm).*

42k

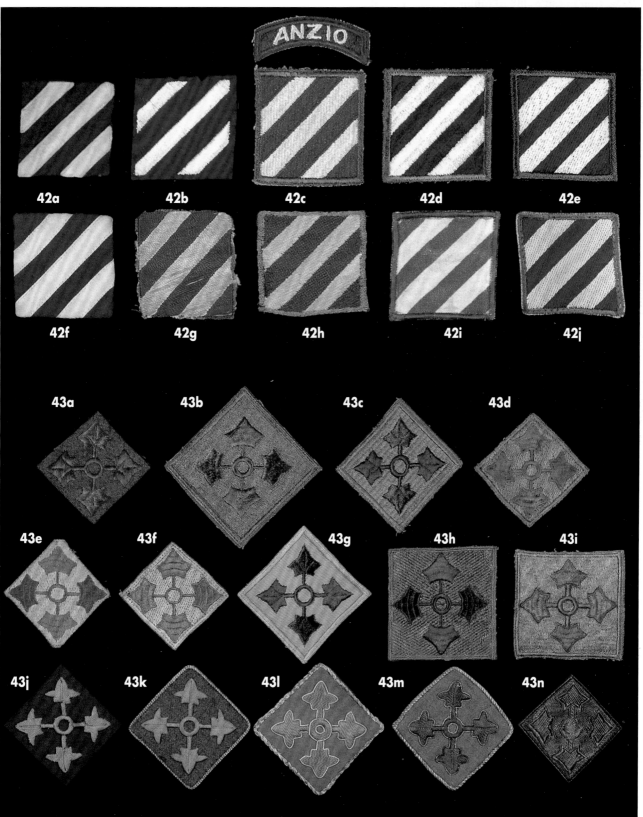

ANZIO

42a 42b 42c 42d 42e

42f 42g 42h 42i 42j

43a 43b 43c 43d

43e 43f 43g 43h 43i

43j 43k 43l 43m 43n

44h *German-made, 1945. Embroidered in bright silver bullion on red felt, strengthened with white twill to reverse. Note that the inscription at the top also exists as a separate tab, embroidered in bullion or white cotton (115 x 67 mm).*

45 - 6th Infantry Division

AC: activated 16 November 1917, under the name of 6th Division, organized 26 November 1917 at Camp McClellan (Alabama). Inactivated 30 September 1921 at Camp Grant (Illinois). Reactivated 10 October 1939 at Fort Lewis (Washington). Re-designated and reorganized 9 April 1942 as 6th Motorized Division. Reorganized and re-designated 21 March 1943 as the 6th Infantry Division. Inactivated 10 January 1949 in Korea.
A: 20 October 1918 by the AEF, confirmed 22 October, then 21 January 1922.
S: six point star for the numeric designation, motif used for the identification of baggage, equipment and vehicles belonging to the division during the Great War, the reason for the choice of red remains unknown. Nickname: 'Red Star Division - The Sightseeing Sixth'.
C: 14▲ - 15▲.

45a *1930-40 manufacture, cut out from red felt (68 x 60 mm).*
45b *Variation 1935-40, fully embroidered (63 x 52 mm).*
45c *Standard WW2 manufacture (63 x 50 mm).*
45d *Variation with olive drab border.*
45e *Variation, green back (74 x 67 mm).*

46 - 7th Infantry Division

AC: activated 6 December 1917, under the name of 7th Division, organized 1 January 1918 at Camp Wheeler (Georgia).

46f

Inactivated 22 September 1918 at Camp Meade (Maryland). Reactivated 1 July 1940 at Camp Ord (California). Reorganized and re-designated 7th Motorized Division 9 April 1942. Reorganized and re-designated 1 January 1943 as the 7th Infantry Division.
A: 23 October 1918 by the AEF. Type with olive drab border approved in January 1943.
S: two interwoven number sevens for the numeric designation, the hourglass shape led to the nickname 'Hourglass Division'.
C: 2▲ - 10 - 13 - 19.

46a *1930-40 manufacture, embroidered on felt, thin black twill to reverse (diameter 69 mm).*
46b *Standard WW2 manufacture, fully embroidered in horizontal stripes, white back (diameter 60 mm).*
46c *Theatre made, perhaps Korean 1945, very fine embroidery, green back (diameter 62 mm).*
46d *So called 'German' type embroidery, 1944-45, olive drab border, white back. The black triangles hug the curve of the patch (diameter 63 mm).*
46e *Variation, green back (diameter 60 mm).*
46f *Theatre made, probably Korean, 1945, red wool background, white twill reinforcing to reverse, border and triangles outlined in thin silver bullion.*

Note: as this unit served during the Korean War (1950-53), then was stationed in South Korea in the 1960s, it is difficult to accurately date theatre made patches.

44 - 5th Infantry Division

AC: activated 17 November 1917 as 5th Division, organized on 11 December at Camp Logan (Texas). Inactivated 4 October 1921 at Camp Jackson (South Carolina). Reactivated on 16 October 1939 at Fort McClellan (Alabama). Reorganized and re-designated 1 August 1942 as 5th Infantry Division.
A: 20 October 1918 by the AEF.
S: the red colour of the artillery in memory of its first commander. The diamond was the marking of the division's baggage, equipment and vehicles during the Great War. Between and 1930 and 1940, a blue number five was embroidered in the centre of the patch without this ever being officially sanctioned. Nickname: 'Red Diamond Division,' 'The Ace of Diamonds.' Motto: "We will."
C: 25 - 26 - 30 - 32 - 34 (Note. The 10th Infantry Regiment was assigned in Iceland in September 1941).

44a *1930-40 manufacture, number embroidered on red felt, thin white gauze to reverse (73 x 62 mm).*
44b *Variation, 1930-40, red felt on olive drab wool (70 x 42 mm)*
44c *1935-40 manufacture, embroidered on olive drab wool (65 x 48 mm)*
44d *Standard WW2 manufacture, fully embroidered (62 x 34 mm)*
44e *Variation, olive drab border and back (73 x 43 mm)*
44f *European made 1944-45, crude embroidery in very thin red thread on thin OD wool, multicolour reverse (green, blue and red) (90 x 47 mm).*
44g *European made 1944-45, silk applied on red wool with overstitched edge, black twill glued to reverse, thick paper sandwiched between the two layers (73 x 49 mm)*

Top.
1945 in Germany, two 5th Division QM officers confer. The unit sign can be seen on the right hand man, as well as on the large road sign in the background.
(National Archives)

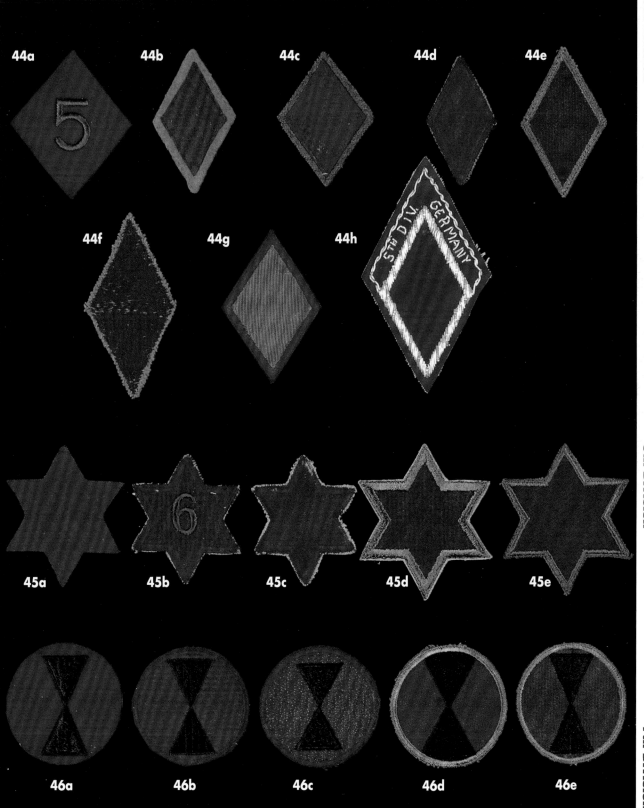

48 - 9th Infantry Division

AC: activated 8 July 1918 under the name of 9th Division. Organized 18 July 1918 and inactivated 15 February 1919 at Camp Sheridan (Alabama). Reorganized 24 March 1923 as the 9th Division. Activated 1 August 1942 as the 9th Infantry Division. Inactivated 15 January 1947 in Germany.
A: 18 November 1925
S: double quatrefoil (heraldic symbol of the ninth son) for the numeric designation. The red and blue are the colours of divisional flags, the unit number in the centre is symbolized by the white disk; these three colours are also those of the national flag. Nickname: 'Varsity, Old Reliable'.
C: 23▲ - 25 - 26 - 30 - 32 - 34 - 36 - 38.

48a *1930-40 manufacture, felt sewn onto olive drab wool (diameter 65 mm).*
48b *1935-40 manufacture, embroidered on olive drab wool with thin outline on the leaves and white disk (diameter: 65 mm).*
48c *Standard WW2 embroidered manufacture, white back (diameter 58 mm).*
48d *Variation, leaves with white borders, thin blue border separating the upper leaves from the bottom leaves (diameter 60 mm).*
48e *Variation, 'German' type embroidery, diameter 58 mm.*
48f *British (?) manufacture, khaki background, outlined white disk, blurred edges on the leaves, white back (diameter: 65 mm).*
48g *European made 1944-45, leaves embroidered in horizontal stripes and thinly outlined in white, brown corduroy base (diameter: 62 mm).*
48h *European made 1944-45, embroidered on thick olive drab wool, white felt backing visible around the edge (diameter: 60 mm).*
48i *Variation, rounded felt leaves, outlined with white stitches, brown wool gabardine background (diameter 57 mm).*
48j *Variation, chain stitch embroidery on black wool, overstitched on edges to prevent fraying (diameter 65 mm).*

49 - 10th Mountain Division

AC: activated 10 July 1943 as the 10th Light Infantry Division (Pack, Alpine), organized 17 July at Camp Hale (Colorado). Re-designated 10th Mountain Division 6 November 1944. Inactivated 30 November 1945 at Camp Carson (Colorado). An earlier 10th Division, formed in August 1918 at Camp Funston (Kansas) was not shipped to France and disbanded on 2 August 1919. It is not considered to be the ancestor of the 10th Mountain Division.
A: no official approval for the 1918 division as it was never part of the AEF. 7 January 1944 for the mountain division patch and 22 November for the 'Mountain' tab.
S: powder keg and crossed bayonets symbolizing the infantry, in the national colours. The crossed bayonets form the Roman ten numeral.
Nickname: 'Mountaineers Division'.
C: 31 - 33.

49a *The division's 1918 patch, 1930-40 manufacture, made for veterans or perhaps even for the collector's market!*
49b *Standard WW2 manufacture, fully embroidered (63 x 52 mm).*
49c *Variation, less detailing on the bayonet grips (62 x 54 mm).*
49d *Standard WW2 manufacture. Italian made tab, embroidered, with brown wool backing.*
49e *Italian made, in one piece, embroidered onto a thin blue twill background reinforced with thick black twill (80 x 60 mm).*

Top left.
10 September 1944, Major General Lawton Collins awards Pfc Edgar L. Fournier with the Distinguished Service Cross. Fournier displays the 9th Division patch on his field jacket sleeve. The 39th Infantry's slogan is painted on his helmet.
(National Archives)

47 - 8th Infantry Division

AC: activated 17 December 1917 as the 8th Division, organized 5 January 1918 at Camp Fremont (California). Inactivated 5 September 1919 at Camp Lee (Virginia). Reorganized 24 March 1923. Reactivated 1 July 1940 at Camp Jackson (South Carolina). Re-designated and reorganized 9 April 1942 as the 8th Motorized Division. Reorganized and re-designated 8th Infantry Division 15 May 1943. Inactivated 20 November 1945 at Fort Leonard Wood (Missouri).
A: 8 April 1919 by the AEF.
S: yellow arrow as a reminder of the unit's nickname and emblem of the explorer Fremont (the unit having been formed in a camp bearing his name). Nicknames: 'The Arrowhead Division-Pathfinder Division.' Motto: "These are my credentials."
C: 26 - 30 - 32 - 34.

47a *1930-40 manufacture, embroidered on blue felt, thin white gauze to reverse (52 x 40 mm).*
47b *Variation, embroidered with blue edge on olive drab wool (70 x 50 mm).*
47c *Variation, embroidered in horizontal stripes (67 x 50 mm).*
47d *Standard WW2 manufacture, green back (65 x 44 mm).*
47e *Variation (60 x 44 mm).*
47f *Variation, olive drab border and back (70 x 44 mm).*
47g *Variation, 'German' type embroidery, white back (67 x 50 mm).*
47h *WW2 manufacture, square top, white back (70 x 47 mm).*
47i *Variation (70 x 52 mm).*
47j *European made, probably French. Chain stitch embroidery on dark blue wool, reinforced on reverse with brown wool. Note the Norman shield shape, rounded at the top and bottom.*

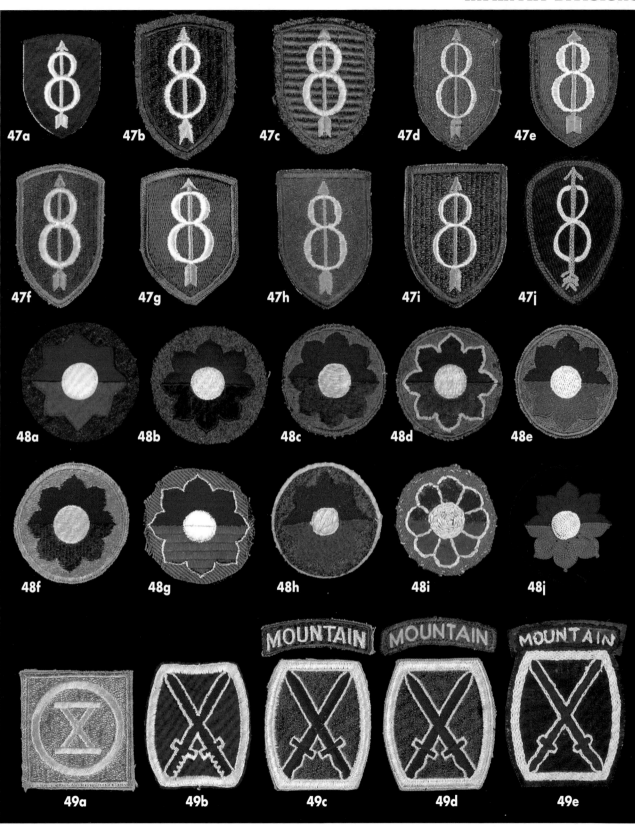

47a
47b
47c
47d
47e

47f
47g
47h
47i
47j

48a
48b
48c
48d
48e

48f
48g
48h
48i
48j

49a
49b
49c
49d
49e

50 - 11th Airborne Division

AC: activated 12 November 1942. Organized 25 February 1943 at Camp Mackall (North Carolina). Note that there is no relation between the 11th Airborne Division and the 11th Division formed in August 1918 and which did not participate in the Great War.
A: 4 January 1943.
S: the three national colours, winged numbers for the numeric designation and the airborne role of the unit. Nickname: 'The Angel Division.
C: 13 - 14▲ - 15.

50a *Standard WW2 manufacture, fully embroidered, separate tab with thick lettering (patch 75 x 55 mm).*
50b *Variation, embroidered in a single piece of khaki twill (95 x 63 mm).*
50c *Variation, note the different design of the wings (95 x 60 mm).*
50d *'Oval' for the divisional HQ, the glider or parachutist badge being pinned over it. The national colours of red, white and blue were also those of HQ units.*
50e *WW2 manufacture, embroidered on blue felt with white reinforcing gauze to reverse, blue border and tab outline (95 x 56 mm).*

51 - 13th Airborne Division

AC: activated 26 December 1942. Organized 13 August 1943 at Fort Bragg (North Carolina). Inactivated 25 February 1946 at the same place. Note that there is no relation between the 13th Airborne Division and the 13th Division formed in July 1918 and which did not see fighting in the Great War.
A: 2 June 1943.
S: the unicorn is the symbol of virtue, courage and strength. The wings symbolize the airborne role, blue is the infantry color and that of the sky from which the unit descends.
C: 26.

51a *Standard WW2 type, fully embroidered in two parts, olive drab border and white back (patch 75 x 54 mm). Tab also standard manufacture with a curve specific to this patch, brown back.*
51b *Variation, single piece, embroidered on khaki twill visible between the shield and the tab, olive drab border (90 x 52 mm).*
51c *Variation, shield with blue border, separation between shield and tab marked by an olive drab border (95 x 52 mm).*
51d *Variation, no separation between the shield and tab (90 x 52 mm).*
51e *Variation (93 x 56 mm).*

52 - 17th Airborne Division

AC: activated 16 December 1942. Organized 15 April 1943 at Camp Mackall (North Carolina). Inactivated 14 September 1945 at Camp Myles Standish (Massachusetts). There is no relation between the 17th Airborne Division and the 17th Division formed in August 1918, but which did not take part in any fighting in the Great War.
A: 8 February 1943.
S: eagle's talon symbolizing attack from the sky, black background indicating the ability to strike at night. Nickname: 'Thunder from Heaven, The Golden Talon Division'.
C: 25 - 26▲ - 34.

52a *Standard WW2 manufacture, embroidered in one piece on khaki twill, visible between the shield and the tab (74 x 60 mm).*
52b *Variation, note that the third talon is turned to the left (75 x 62 mm).*
52c *Standard WW2 manufacture, in two parts, the lemon yellow colour tone has been replaced by golden yellow (73 x 60 mm).*
52d *Variation, inverted talon, unauthorized patch designed to be worn on the right arm (Combat patch).*
52e *Standard WW2 manufacture, golden yellow talon and lemon yellow tab (diameter 62 mm).*
52f *Variation, inverted talon, ditto 52b (diameter 56 mm).*
52g *British (?) manufacture 1944-45, inverted talon, ditto 52b/f, black back, oval shape (61 x 52 mm). Classic manufacture tab. We surmise that tabs in the same manufacture as the patch must have been made, the latter was found with the tab shown.*
52h *European made 1944-45, negative motif to reverse, sometimes identified as Italian. Olive drab border, same manufacture tab.*
52i *European made 1944-45, gold bullion embroidery on a thick paper-stiffened black backing. This patch was found without a tab, although we can suppose that the latter was of the same type.*
52j *European made 1944-45, thick cotton embroidery on black wool, black border, over an olive drab wool base, black twill glued to reverse (75 x 66 mm).*

THE TALON Crosses the Rhine

PUBLICATION OF THE SEVENTEENTH AIRBORNE DIVISION

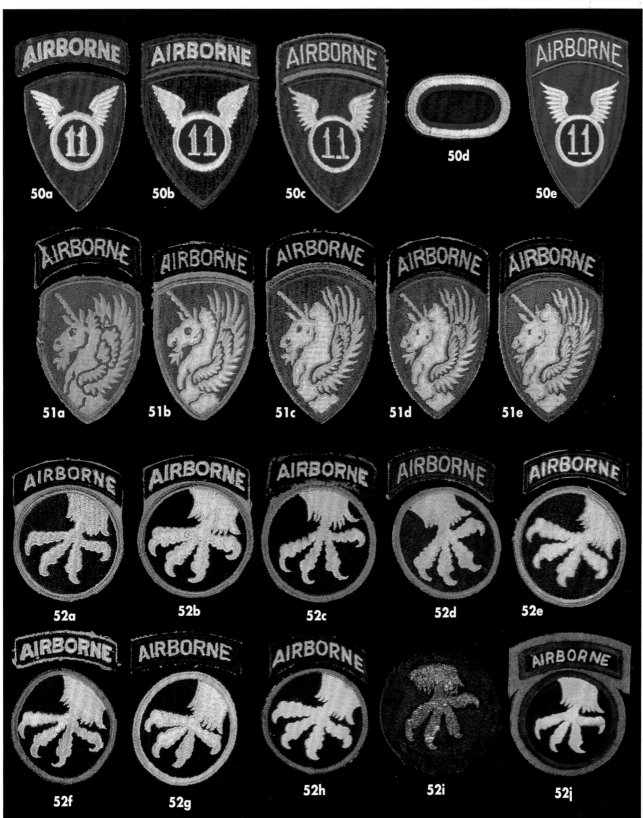

50a

50b

50c

50d

50e

51a

51b

51c

51d

51e

52a

52b

52c

52d

52e

52f

52g

52h

52i

52j

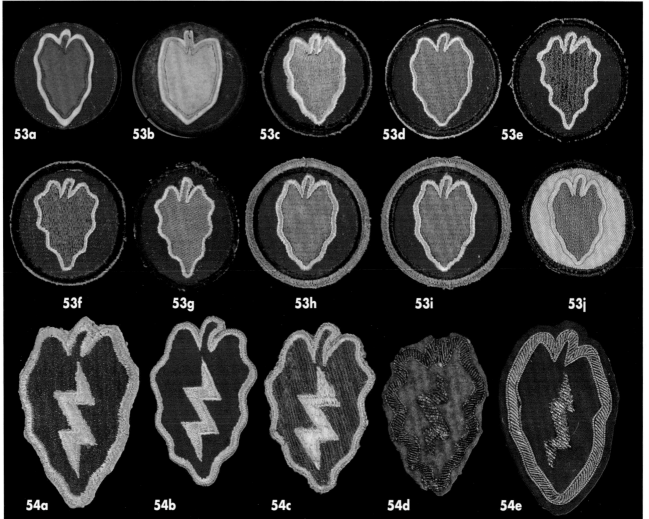

53a 53b 53c 53d 53e
53f 53g 53h 53i 53j
54a 54b 54c 54d 54e

53 - 24th Infantry Division

AC: activated 1 February 1921 as the Hawaiian Division. Organized 1 March 1921 at Schofield Barracks (Territory of Hawaii). Reorganized and re-designated 1 October 1941 as 24th Infantry Division.
A: patch authorized for the Hawaiian Division 9 September 1921. Approved in August 1941.
S: the Taro leaf (a plant from the Hawaiian islands) is a reminder of where the unit was raised and garrisoned. The red and yellow colours are those of the former kings of these islands, as well as those of the Spanish kingdom that once ruled these islands. Nickname: 'Victory Division,' originating from the victory parade in Leyte (Philippines) in August 1945.
C: 6 - 13▲ - 14 - 15▲ - 20s.

53a *1920-30 manufacture, sewn-on felt.*
53b *Locally made 1920-30, attached to a metal plate fitted with a pin, that allows the patch to be removed. This device, known as the 'No-So Shoulder patch,' and patented in February 1924, was made in Hawaii.*
53c *Standard WW2 manufacture, fully embroidered (diameter 54 mm).*
53d *Variation, white back (diameter 57 mm).*

53e *Variation (diameter 57 mm).*
53f *Variation, black back (diameter 57 mm).*
53g *Variation, 'German' type embroidery (60 x 53 mm), patch is misshapen due to washing the garment.*
53h *WW2 manufacture, olive drab border, white back (diameter 62 mm).*
53i *Variation, green back (diameter 65 mm).*
53j *Theatre made 1945, probably in the Philippines, embroidery on silk background, black silk braid around the edge. There are many variations in the shape of the leaf. As with other divisions that later served in Korea, it's very difficult to accurately date the many locally/theater made patches seen.*

54 - 25th Infantry Division

AC: activated 26 August 1941. Organized 1 October 1941 at Schofield Barracks (Territory of Hawaii).
A: 25 September 1944.
S: the Taro leaf is a reminder of where the unit was organized. The lightning bolt suggests the will to strike. Red and yellow are the colours of Spain, the former ruling power of the archipelago, until the Spanish-American War of 1898. Nicknames: 'Tropic Lightning Division, Pineapple Division'.
C: 6 - 11 - 14 - 16.

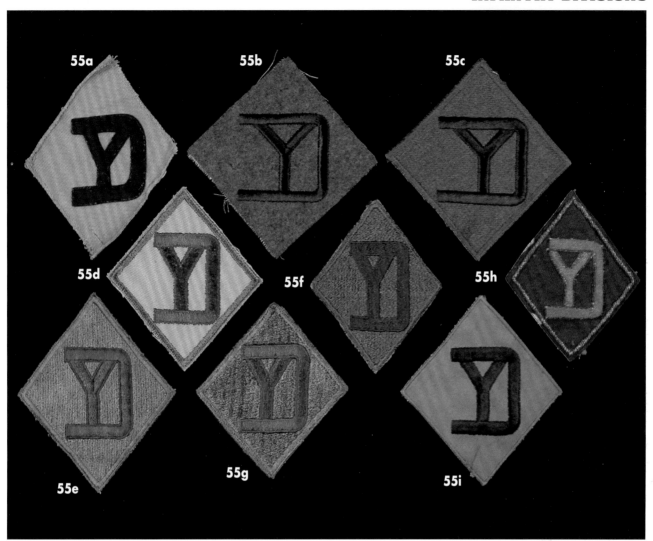

54a *Standard WW2 manufacture (75 x 50 mm).*
54b *Variation, 'German' type embroidery (65 x 44 mm).*
54c *Variation (67 x 44 mm).*
54d *Theatre made, probably Japanese 1945, gold bullion on red felt, stock backing (54 x 43 mm).*
54e *Variation, white reinforcing twill to reverse (76 x 48 mm).*
As this division served later in Korea, it is difficult to accurately date its theatre made patches.

55 - 26th Infantry Division

AC: activated 18 July 1917 in the National Guard
as the 26th Division, organized 22 August 1917 in
Boston (Massachusetts). Inactivated 3 May 1919 at Camp Devens
(Massachusetts). Reorganized 21 March 1929 in the Massachusetts
National Guard. Federalized on 16 January 1941. Reorganized and
re-designated 26th Infantry Division 12 February 1942. Inactivated
29 December 1945 at Camp Myles Standish (Massachusetts).
A: 26 October 1918 by the AEF, confirmed in October 1935.
S: the initials YD of the unit's nickname ('Yankee Division')
in infantry blue.
C: 25 - 26 - 32 - 34.

55a *1930-40 manufacture for the summer uniform, dark blue felt letters sewn onto khaki twill, oversewn border. The same type exists for the winter uniform, on olive drab wool.*
55b *1935-40 manufacture, embroidered on olive drab wool, thin white gauze to reverse (110 x 108 mm).*
55c *Variation, embroidered on officer's Olive Drab Shade 51 gabardine.*
55d *Patch for the summer uniform, 1935-40, on khaki twill, olive drab border, gauze glued to reverse (100 x 88 mm).*
55e *Standard WW2 manufacture, fully embroidered, white back (110 x 90 mm).*
55f *Variation (96 x 85 mm).*
55g *Variation, 'German' type embroidery (95 x 73 mm).*
55h *European made, embroidered in blue silk highlighted with gold thread, silver bullion border, khaki felt background, thick white reinforcing twill to reverse (94 x 76 mm).*
55i *Variation, dark blue embroidery on very thin green khaki twill, thin merrowed border in same colour shade, thin white gauze to reverse (104 x 94 mm).*

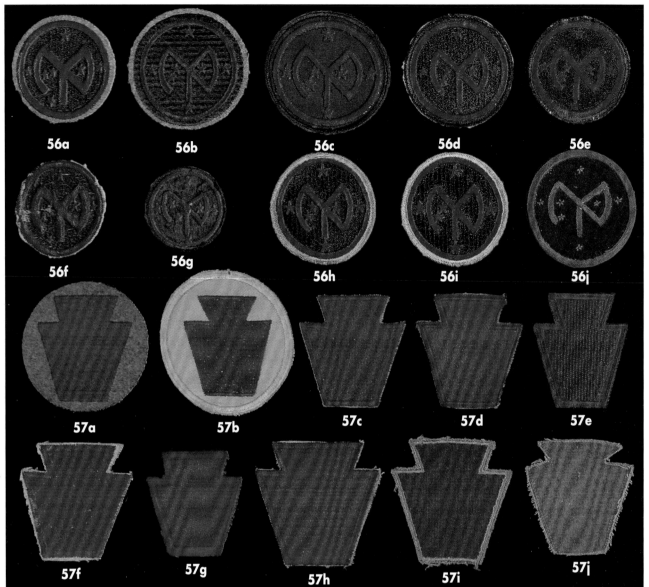

56 - 27th Infantry Division

AC: the first National Guard unit to be mobilized as a division in order to fight along the Mexican border in 1916, under the name of 6th Division. Reorganized at Camp Wadsworth (South Carolina) 18 July 1917, as the 27th Division.
Federalized 15 October 1940. Re-designated 27th Infantry Division 1 September 1942. Inactivated 31 December 1945 at Camp Lawton (Washington State).
A: 29 October 1918 by the AEF.
S: the letters N and Y symbolize the state of New York where the unit was formed during the Great War. The stars evoke the Orion constellation in honor of its 1918 commander, Major General John F. O'Ryan. Nickname: 'New York Division'.
C: 6 - 19▲ - 21.

56a 1930-40 manufacture, motif embroidered on olive drab wool, white back. The lowest star is to the left of the letter Y (diameter 60 mm).
56b Variation, black back (diameter 70 mm).
56c 1930-45 manufacture, motif embroidered on black twill, merrowed border in same colour, thin black gauze to reverse (diameter 72 mm).
56d Standard WW2 manufacture, fully embroidered, white back (diameter 63 mm).
56e Variation, green back (diameter 58 mm).
56f Theatre made, perhaps Australian, smaller stars than those on 56A (diameter 50 mm).
56g Variation 56e, 'German' type embroidery (diameter 47 mm).
56h WW2 manufacture with olive drab border, white back (diameter 60 mm).
56i Variation, note the absence of the star situated at the centre of the N and Y letters in the right-hand side of the patch (diameter 60 mm).
56j VPacific theatre made, red cotton embroidery on black felt, twill glued to reverse (diameter 63 mm).

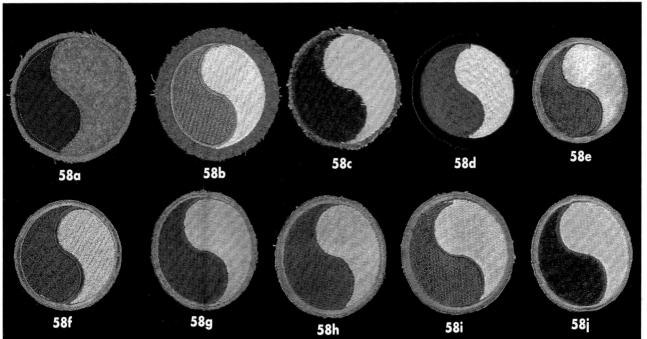

58a   58b   58c   58d   58e

58f   58g   58h   58i   58j

57 - 28th Infantry Division

AC: constituted with various elements of the Pennsylvania National Guard on 29 June 1916, in Mount Gretna, under the name of 7th Division. Activated 15 July 1917 and organized 18 July at Camp Hancock (Georgia). Re-designated 28th Division 1 September 1917. Inactivated at Camp Dix (New Jersey) 17 May 1919. Reorganized 22 December 1921 as a Pennsylvanian National Guard unit. Called up for federal service 17 February 1941. Reorganized and re-designated 28th Infantry Division 17 February 1942. Inactivated 13 December 1945 at Camp Shelby (Mississippi).

A: 19 October 1918 by the AEF. Approved in November 1918.

S: The keystone, symbol of the State of Pennsylvania. Nicknames: 'Keystone Division, Bloody Bucket.' Motto: "Roll on."

C: 25 - 26 - 30 - 32 - 34.

57a *1930-40 manufacture, insignia embroidered on olive drab wool (diameter 40 mm).*
57b *Variation for the summer uniform, embroidered on khaki twill, merrowed border in same colour, white gauze to reverse (diameter 73 mm).*
57c *Standard WW2 manufacture, fully embroidered, white back (59 x 57 mm).*
57d *Variation, green back (60 x 58 mm).*
57e *Variation, black back (60 x 50 mm).*
57f *Variation, white back (61 x 57 mm).*
57g *Variation, 'German' type embroidery, red reverse, very thick outer border (55 x 53 mm).*
57h *Variation, embroidered in horizontal stripes (65 x 68 mm).*
57i *WW2 manufacture with olive drab border and reverse (65 x 65 mm).*
57j *European manufacture, 1944-45, thin piece of red cloth sewn onto grey-green wool (60 x 58 mm).*
57k *Above, this patch, identical to 57h, was for a long time thought to have been a variation, modified by cutting off the keystone's upper tips and by adding a merrowed border once cut. This oddity was actually made for the movie "Because you're mine" in the 1950s.*

57k

58 - 29th Infantry Division

AC: activated in July 1917 with National Guard units from Delaware, Maryland, New Jersey, Virginia and the District of Columbia, at Camp McClellan (Alabama), under the name of 8th Division. Re-designated 29th Division 25 August 1917. Organized in September 1917. Federalized 3 February 1941. Reorganized and re-designated 29th Infantry Division 12 March 1942. Inactivated 17 January 1946 at Camp Kilmer (New Jersey).

A: 21 October 1918 by the AEF. Authorized in November 1918.

S: the blue and gray is a reference to the unit's nickname, originating from the unit having men from states that fought for both sides during the Civil War, the Union soldiers mostly wore blue uniforms whereas those of the Confederate army wore gray. The design is based on the Buddhist yin-yang symbol for reasons that remain unknown. Nickname: 'The Blue and Gray Division.' Motto: "29th Let's go!"

C: 26 - 30▲ - 32 - 34.

58a *1930-35 manufacture, two pieces of felt sewn onto olive drab wool (diameter 68 mm).*
58b *1930-40 manufacture, embroidered on olive drab wool with thin stripe around the circle and between the two colours, thin white gauze to reverse (diameter 67 mm).*
58c *Variation, black back (diameter 60 mm).*
58d *Variation, embroidered on dark blue wool (diameter 60 mm).*
58e *Standard WW2 manufacture, olive drab border, white back, thin stripe between the two colours (diameter 52 mm).*
58f *Variation (diameter 57 mm).*
58g *Variation (diameter 58 mm).*
58h *Variation, green back (diameter 62 mm).*
58i *Variation, white back (diameter 61 mm).*
58j *Manufacture known as 'British type,' black back, very light olive drab border.*

59 - 30th Infantry Division

AC: activated 18 July 1917 with National Guard units from North and South Carolina, Tennessee and Georgia, under the name of 9th National Guard Division. With the troops assembled 3 August 1917, the unit was designated as the 30th Division. Organized 28 August to 12 September 1917 at Fort Sevier (South Carolina). Inactivated 7 May 1919 at Camp Jackson (South Carolina). Reorganized 24 August 1926 in Atlanta (Georgia). Called up for federal service on 16 September 1940 at Fort Jackson (South Carolina). Reorganized and re-designated 30th Infantry Division 16 February 1942. Inactivated 25 November 1945 at Fort Jackson (South Carolina).

A: 23 October 1918 by the AEF.

S: the design forms the letters O and H, the initials of the unit's nickname, "Old Hickory," in honor of the general and US president, Andrew Jackson, also the Roman numeral 30 in the centre.

C: 25 - 26 - 30 - 32 - 34.

Up to the end of the 1930s, the patch was worn horizontally and is shown this way in many period publications. It was worn vertically during WW2, something that is logical given its design.

59a *1930-40 manufacture, embroidered on olive drab wool, with a PX label from Camp Atterbury (Indiana) where the unit stationed from November 1943 to January 1944. The soldier trimmed the square border before sewing on the patch.*
59b *Standard WW2 manufacture, 'German' type manufacture, identical to fig. a but that has been trimmed. Thicker numbers (64 x 42 mm).*
59c *Manufacture known as 'British,' black back (57 x 41 mm).*
59d *Variation, double blue border (70 x 50 mm).*
59e *European made, embroidered with thick thread on olive drab wool.*
59f *Red border, often associated with divisional artillery.*
59g *Variation, manufacture known as 'British,' black back (64 x 43 mm).*
59h *Variation, European tailor made, embroidered with blue cotton enhanced with silver bullion on the border and letter O, red felt background, thick white reinforcing twill and paper glued to reverse (48 mm).*
59i *WW2 manufacture with olive drab border, lighter blue, white back (58 x 43 mm).*
59j *Variation, 59 x 45 mm.*

60 - 31st Infantry Division

AC: activated 18 July 1917 under the name of 10th National Guard Division. Organized 25 August 1917 at Camp Wheeler (Georgia), took the name of 31st Division. Inactivated 14 February 1919 at Camp Gordon (Georgia). Reactivated in 1923 by re-designation of the 39th Division. Reorganized 15 February 1924 at St. Augustine (Florida). Called up for federal service 25 November 1940 at Camp Blanding (Florida). Reorganized and re-designated 31st Infantry Division 27 February 1942. Inactivated 21 December 1945 at Camp Stoneman (California).

A: 7 March 1919 by the AEF.

S: two back to back D letters for the 'Dixie Division' nickname. Dixieland designates the territory situated beneath the Mason-Dixon Line. During the Civil War, most of its men came from Alabama, Florida and Georgia. Motto: "It will be done."

C: 15▲- 20 - 21.

Machine embroidery of regulation shoulder sleeve insignia

These two photos allow us to understand the manufacturing process of regulation shoulder sleeve insignia (seen here are those of the 31st Infantry Division and the 4th Armored Division). Once the roll was fully embroidered by the machine, the patches were machine cut out and, perhaps, with less well equipped manufacturers, by hand. The base material, more often khaki twill, could also be in a colour similar to that of the patch's border (red, blue, black etc.)

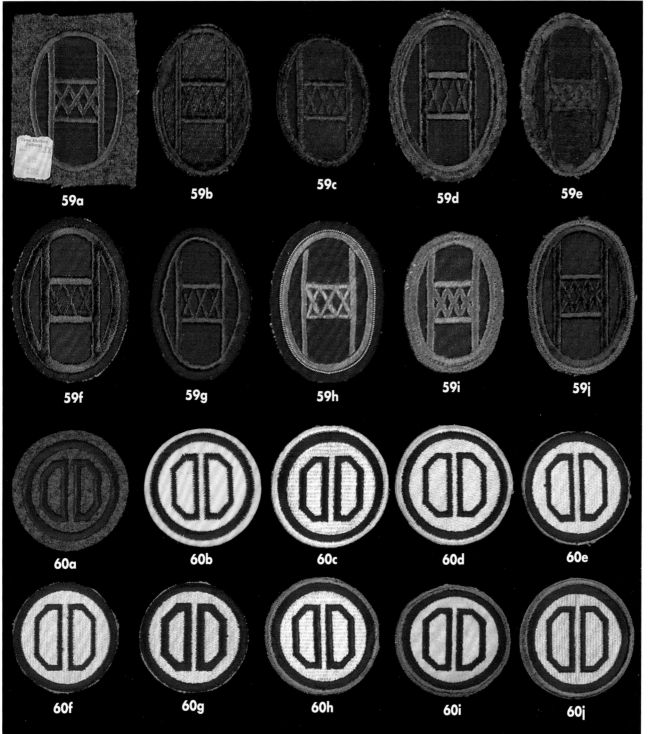

59a 59b 59c 59d 59e

59f 59g 59h 59i 59j

60a 60b 60c 60d 60e

60f 60g 60h 60i 60j

60a *1930-35 manufacture, red embroidery on olive drab wool, thin black reinforcing twill to reverse (diameter 70 mm).*
60b *Variation, 1935-40, white felt background, white gauze to reverse (diameter 68 mm).*
60c *Standard WW2 manufacture, fully embroidered (diameter 68 mm).*
60d *Variation (diameter 70 mm).*

60e *Variation (diameter 64 mm).*
60f *Variation, green back (diameter 62 mm).*
60g *Variation, thin border around the letters (diameter 63 mm).*
60h *WW2 manufacture, olive drab border, white back (diameter 67 mm).*
60i *Variation, green back.*
60j *Variation, white back.*

61 - 32nd Infantry Division

AC: activated 18 July 1917 as the 11th National Guard Division. Redesignated 26 August at Camp MacArthur (Tennessee) as the 32nd Division. Reorganized 24 July 1924 in Lansing (Michigan) in the Michigan and Wisconsin National Guard. Called up for federal service on 15 October 1940. Reorganized and re-designated 32nd Infantry Division 1 July 1942. Inactivated 28 February 1946 in Japan.

A: 11 November 1918 by the AEF.

S: designed supposedly by General William Haan, the Division's commander in 1918: "I chose the line shot through with the arrow because we had broken through all of the Hun defenses." Nicknames: 'The Red Arrow Division, Les Terribles'.

C: 14 - 15 - 20.

61a *1930-35 manufacture, felt on olive drab wool (arrow: 80 x 30 mm).*
61b *Variation, very thin red felt (85 x 28 mm).*
61c *1935-40 manufacture, embroidered on olive drab wool, thin border on the arrow (80 x 30 mm).*

61d *Variation, rounded top, as with the patch used at the end of the Great War, thin white reinforcing cloth to reverse (65 x 18 mm).*
61e *Standard WW2 manufacture, red border (83 x 33 mm).*
61f *Variation (88 x 40 mm).*
61g *WW2 manufacture with green border and back (92 x 35 mm).*
61h *Variation, white back (85 x 37 mm).*
61i *Variation, embroidery in horizontal stripes (90 x 38 mm).*
61j *Theatre made, perhaps Philippine, 1945, with black border, reinforcing paper glued to reverse (90 x 28 mm).*
61k *Theatre made 1945, thin red silk on khaki twill (80 x 32 mm).*
61l *Theatre made 1945, thin red silk red and white sewn on black wool (76 x 32 mm).*

62 - 33rd Infantry Division

AC: activated 18 July 1917 under the name of 12th National Guard Division. Redesignated 27 August 1917 at Camp Logan (Tennessee) as 33rd Division. Inactivated at Camp Grant (Illinois) 6 June 1919. Reorganized 13 December 1923 in the Illinois National Guard. Called up for federal service 5 May 1941. Reorganized and re-designated 33rd Infantry Division 21 February 1942. Inactivated 5 February 1946 in Japan.

A: 21 October 1918 by the AEF.

S: the yellow cross was the marking used for the identification of baggage and equipment of one of the regiments when it took part in operations in the Philippines in 1898, it was retained for the division of 1918. Other sources state that this marking was chosen as it identified gas shells that were not to be tampered with. Nicknames: 'The Illinois Division, The Prairie Division'.

C: 14 -15.

62a *1925-35 manufacture, two pieces of felt on olive drab wool (diameter 70 mm).*
62b *1930-40 manufacture, embroidered on black felt in horizontal stripes (diameter 52 mm).*
62c *Variation, embroidered on an olive drab wool shield (73 x 60 mm).*
62d *Standard WW2 manufacture, border around the cross and the sides if the shield (diameter 60 mm).*
62e *Variation, very thin borders, embroidery in horizontal and vertical waves (diameter 62 mm).*
62f *Variation, 'German' type embroidery (57 x 53 mm).*
62g *WW2 manufacture with olive drab border, embroidery in waves (same as 62e), white back (diameter 57 mm).*
62h *Variation, green edge and reverse (diameter 60 mm).*
62i *Tailor made, circa 1935-40, gold bullion embroidery on black wool, all sewn onto olive drab wool.*
62j *Theatre made, no doubt Philippine from 1945, bright gold bullion on black silk.*

1940 pattern service coat altered as an M-1944 Field Jacket ('Ike' Jacket) for a Private First Class in the 29th Infantry Division. Ribbon bar for the American Defense Service Medal, American Campaign Medal, European-African-Middle Eastern Campaign Medal (with a single campaign star device).
– Lower left sleeve: five overseas stripes
– Above left pocket, Combat Infantryman Badge (coherent with the Infantry collar disk)
– Pinned on pocket Marksman shooting badge with Rifle and Pistol qualification bars.
– Above right hand pocket: honorable discharge insignia ('Ruptured Duck') and Distinguished Unit Citation blue and gold ribbon.
(Author's collection)

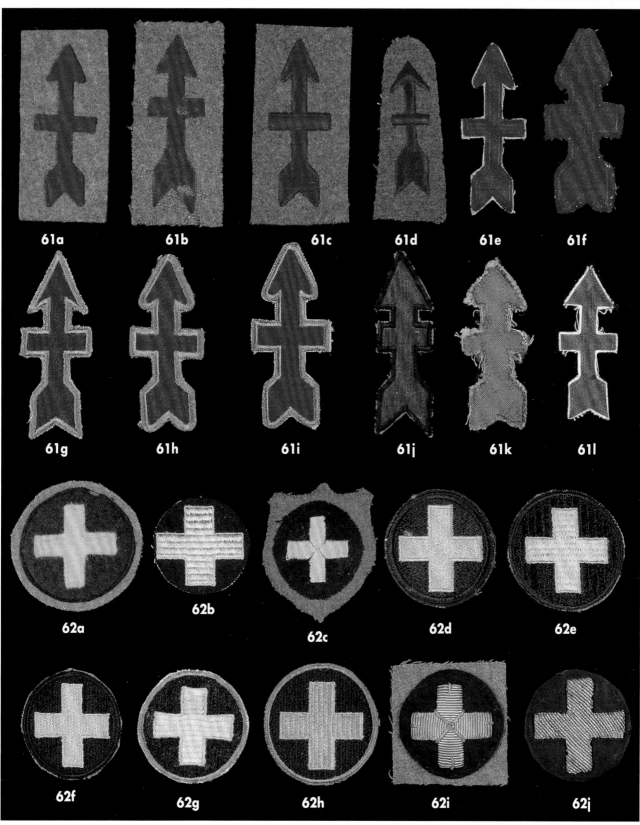

61a 61b 61c 61d 61e 61f

61g 61h 61i 61j 61k 61l

62a 62b 62c 62d 62e

62f 62g 62h 62i 62j

INFANTRY DIVISIONS

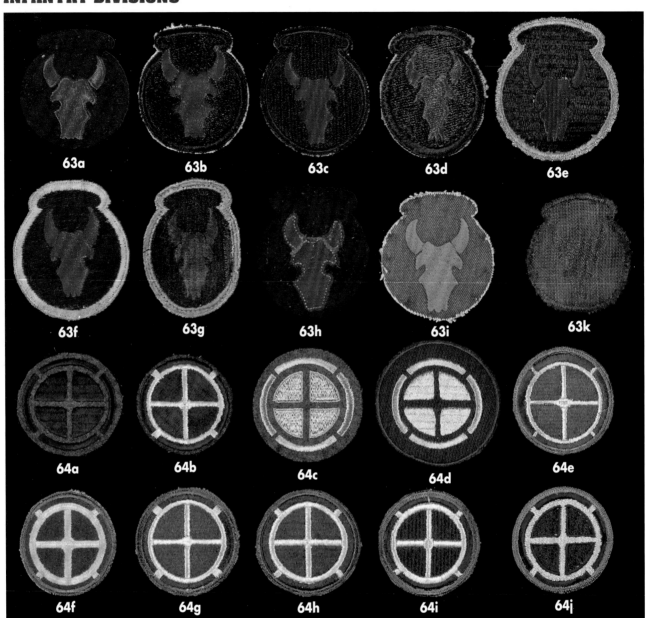

63 - 34th Infantry Division

AC: activated 15 July 1917 under the name of 13th National Guard Division. Organized at Camp Cody (New Mexico) 17 October 1917, took the name of 34th Division. Inactivated 18 February 1919 at Camp Grant (Illinois). Reactivated at the beginning of the 1920s. Federalized and reactivated 10 February 1941 in Council Bluffs (Iowa). Re-designated 34th Infantry Division 31 January 1942 in Northern Ireland. Inactivated 3 November 1945 at Camp Patrick Henry (Virginia).
A: 29 October 1918 by the AEF.
S: the shape represents an Olla (Mexican water jug) and is a reminder of where the unit was raised. The steer skull symbolizes the Middle west states (Iowa, Minnesota, North and South Dakota National Guard).

Nickname: 'The Red Bull Division.' Motto: "Attack, Attack, Attack!"
C: 24 - 29 - 31 - 33 - 35 - 38. The 34th Division has the highest number of days in combat (500) in Europe.

63a *1935-40 manufacture, embroidered on black felt (53 x 50 mm).*
63b *Standard WW2 manufacture, fully embroidered, white back (56 x 50 mm).*
63c *Variation, green back (58 x 50 mm).*
63d *Variation, black back (58 x 48 mm).*
63e *Standard WW2 manufacture, olive drab border, white back, embroidery of black background in horizontal stripes (63 x 56 mm).*
63f *Variation, lighter border, black back (61 x 53 mm).*
63g *Variation, olive drab border, black back (61 x 45 mm).*

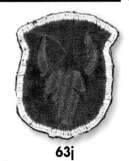

63j

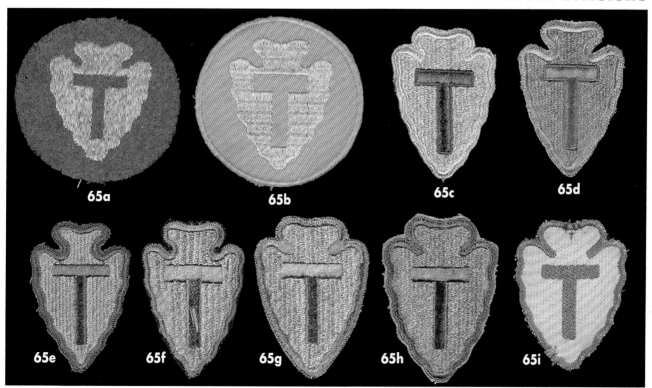

65a   65b   65c   65d

65e   65f   65g   65h   65i

63h *Theatre made in felt, circa 1940/42 (58 x 50 mm).*
63i *Probably British made, printed on black twill, white back, circa 1943-44, (56 x 50 mm).*
63j *Theatre made, probably Italian, designed to be worn on the garrison cap or service coat. Red embroidery on black silk with another ply of black silk to the reverse.*
63k *Woven theatre made, identified as Italian by several American authors, negative of motif on reverse (56 x 48 mm).*
Note: there are several variations in the shape of the steer's head.

64 - 35th Infantry Division

AC: activated 18 July 1917, under the name of 14th National Guard Division. Redesignated 26 August 1917 at Camp Doniphan (Oklahoma) as the 35th Division. Inactivated 26 May 1919 at Camp Funston (Kansas). Reorganized at the beginning of the nineteen-twenties, then once more on 13 September 1935 in Kansas City (Missouri). Federalized on 23 December 1940 (Kansas, Missouri, and Nebraska National Guard). Reorganized and re-designated 35th Infantry Division 1 March 1942. Inactivated 7 December 1945 at Camp Breckinridge (Kentucky).
A: 29 October 1918 by the AEF.
S: the Santa Fe cross was an emblem used to mark the famous trail that led to this town and which was instrumental in the conquest of the Wild West. This symbol was chosen as a reminder of where the unit trained and for its nickname, the 'Santa-Fe Division'.
C: 25 - 26 - 30 - 32 - 34.

It should be noted that during the First World War, a combination of colored triangles, 23 in all, was used to identify the various units of the division.

64a *1935-40, embroidered on olive drab wool (diameter 57 mm).*
64b *Variation, standard blue and white motif embroidered on olive drab wool.*
64c *Variation, thin edges around the triangles, thin black twill to reverse (diameter 60 mm).*
64d *Variation, embroidered on Olive Drab Shade 51 officer gabardine (exists*

also on enlisted men's wool, as well as the khaki cotton of the summer uniform).
64e *Standard WW2 manufacture, fully embroidered, olive drab edge and filling yarn to reverse (diameter 55 mm).*
64f *Variation, khaki back (diameter 55 mm).*
64g *Variation, white back (diameter 54 mm).*
64h *Variation (diameter 57 mm).*
64i *Variation, 'German' type embroidery, khaki border, white back.*
64j *Variation, khaki border (diameter 55 mm).*

65 - 36th Infantry Division

AC: activated at Camp Bowie (Texas) 18 July 1917, under the name of 15th National Guard Division. Organized 17 August 1917 as the 36th Division. Inactivated at Camp Bowie 26 June 1919. Federalized 25 November 1940 from the Texas National Guard. Reorganized and re-designated 36th Infantry Division 1 February 1942. Inactivated at Camp Patrick Henry (Virginia) 15 December 1945.
A: 12 November 1918 by the AEF.
S: The arrowhead shape symbolizes the Indians and where the unit was formed, as well as the letter T for Texas. Nickname: 'The Texas Division'.
C: 24 - 29▲ - 34 - 35 - 36s.

65a *1930-40, embroidered on olive drab wool (diameter 73 mm).*
65b *Variation on khaki twill for the summer uniform, thin white gauze to reverse.*
65c *Standard WW2 manufacture, fully embroidered (65 x 45 mm).*
65d *Variation, more intense blue (65 x 45 mm).*
65e *Standard WW2 manufacture, with olive drab border, 'German' type embroidery, without border around the T (63 x 43 mm).*
65f *Variation, embroidered in horizontal stripes (65 x 45 mm).*
65g *Variation in colours (68 x 50 mm).*
65h *Variation (72 x 50 mm).*
65i *Manufacture known as Italian, woven with the negative of the design to reverse 1944-45 (64 x 48 mm).*

AC: activated in August 1917 under the name of 16th National Guard Division. Organized 3 August 1917 at Camp Sheridan (Alabama). Inactivated upon returning from France. Reorganized 31 May 1923 in Columbus in the Ohio National Guard, took the name of 37th Division. Federalized on 15 October 1940. Re-designated 37th Infantry Division 1 February 1942. Inactivated at Camp Anza (California) 10 December 1945.

A: 5 November 1918 by the AEF.

S: the red and white circles originate from the Ohio flag, which goes by the name of Buckeye State. Nickname: 'The Buckeye Division'.

C: 14▲ - 16.

66a *1925-35 manufacture, two pieces of sewn felt (diameter 63 mm).*
66b *1935-40 variation, embroidered on olive drab wool, thin black gauze to back (diameter 61 mm).*
66c *Standard WW2 manufacture, fully embroidered, thin border around the red circle and the edge (diameter 57 mm).*
66d *Variation, without border (diameter 54 mm).*
66e *Variation, white border, red embroidery in vertical waves, green back (diameter 56 mm).*
66f *Variation (diameter 60 mm).*
66g *Variation (diameter 65 mm).*
66h *Standard WW2 manufacture with olive drab border and thin border around the red circle, white back (diameter 57 mm).*
66i *Variation, without border around red circle, green back (diameter 62 mm).*
66j *Theatre made, probably Philippine circa 1945, red embroidery on thick white twill glue to reverse (diameter 55 mm).*

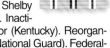

AC: activated 18 July 1917 as 17th National Guard Division. Organized 25 August 1917 at Camp Shelby (Mississippi) and redesignated 38th Division. Inactivated 8 August 1919 at Camp Zachary Taylor (Kentucky). Reorganized 16 March 1923 in Indianapolis (Indiana National Guard). Federalized 17 January 1941 from the Indiana, Kentucky and West Virginia National Guard. Reorganized and re-designated 38th Infantry Division 1 March 1942. Inactivated 9 November 1945 at Camp Anza (California).

A: 30 October 1918 by the AEF.

S: the initials C and Y of the nickname 'Cyclone Division' on the blue and red background of a divisions' field flag. Cyclone was used in reference to a violent storm which destroyed the unit's camp when it was training in 1917. Other nickname: 'The Avengers of Bataan Division'.

C: 14▲ - 15 - 20.

67a *1930-40 manufacture, embroidered on OD wool, black back.*
67b *Standard WW2 manufacture, OD border and back (70 x 60 mm).*
67c *Variation, blue and red embroidery in horizontal stripes. An 'Avengers of Bataan' purportedly existed, its colours are unknown.*

Tie pin for veterans of the 38th Infantry Division.

Wearing Army insignia on the uniform

Shoulder sleeve insignia was worn at the top of the left sleeve, 1.27cm (1/2 inch) from the shoulder seam. In practice it was sometimes sewn on lower down. In 1944, veterans transferred to another division were authorized to wear the patch of the unit that they had previously served with at the top of the right sleeve ('Combat patch'). Patches were worn in regulation fashion on the following garments:
– For officers: on the service coat (khaki and OD), shirt (when worn without a coat), field uniform, wool overcoat and occasionally the raincoat.
– For enlisted men: the service coat (then the M-1944 wool jacket), shirt when worn without a coat, overcoat, field uniform.

NOTE The Meritorious Unit Citation was a collective award for certain support units. Overseas stripes: one stripe = 6 months. Service Stripes: one stripe for three years of federal service.

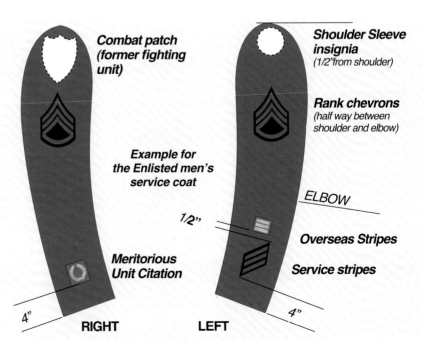

Combat patch (former fighting unit)

Example for the Enlisted men's service coat

Meritorious Unit Citation

RIGHT

4"

Shoulder Sleeve insignia (1/2"from shoulder)

Rank chevrons (half way between shoulder and elbow)

ELBOW

1/2"

Overseas Stripes

Service stripes

LEFT

4"

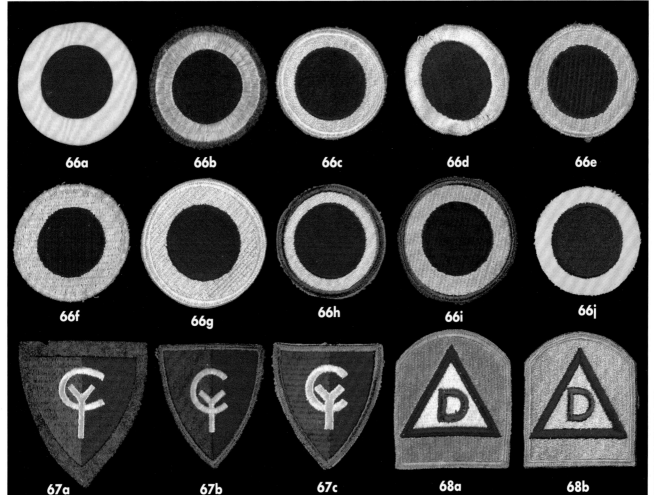

66a 66b 66c 66d 66e

66f 66g 66h 66i 66j

67a 67b 67c 68a 68b

68 - 39th Infantry Division

68a *Standard WW2 manufacture, fully embroidered with a thin border on the letter D and red triangle (75 x 65 mm).*
68b *Variation, lighter gray background, without border, thinner letter (67 x 63 mm).*

AC: activated 18 July 1917 as the 18th National Guard Division. Organized 5 August 1917 at Camp Beauregard (Louisiana), took the name of 39th Division. Depot unit as a source of replacements for other divisions, it did not see combat as a unit. Inactivated 23 January 1919 at Camp Beauregard (Louisiana). Reactivated in 1920 in the National Guard (Alabama, Florida, Mississippi and Louisiana). Organized in 1922, then re-designated 31st Division in 1923. The 39th was not reactivated during World War Two and was only assigned to the National Guard on 30 September 1946.

A: 8 February 1922, this pattern replaced that worn in non-regulation fashion in 1918-19.

S: the letter D and triangle (Delta in the ancient Greek alphabet) evokes the division's nickname. The gray background is for the Confederate troops and the origin of the unit's men. Nickname: 'The Delta Division,' as the unit, when organized in 1917, was made up of recruits from the States along the Mississippi and its delta.

Although the unit did not exist in WW2, its patch was probably made all the same just in case it was reactivated.

69 - 40th Infantry Division

AC: activated 18 July 1917 as the 19th National Guard Division. Organized 15 August 1917 at Camp Kearny (California) as the 40th Division. Inactivated 20 April 1919. Reorganized in Berkeley 18 June 1926 in the California National Guard. Called up for federal service 3 March 1941. Reorganized and re-designated 40th Infantry Division 18 February 1942. Inactivated 7 April 1946 at Camp Stoneman (California).

A: 23 November 1918 by the AEF.

S: the sun and twelve rays symbolizing the south-western states, from which the men came from when the division was organized in the Great War. The blue background is for the sky, the Pacific Ocean and the colour of the infantry. Nicknames: 'The Sunshine Division - The Sunburst Division'.

C: 3 - 14▲ - 20. Originally worn as a square, the patch was sewn positioned on its point during WW2.

69a *1935–40 manufacture, lemon yellow embroidery on dark blue wool, green back (58 x 58 mm).*
69b *Variation, golden yellow embroidery, cut out in a rectangular shape (55 x 9 mm).*
69c *Variation, royal blue felt background, lemon yellow embroidery (69 x 63 mm).*
69d *Variation, blue-gray background (63 x 63 mm).*
69e *Variation, cut out in a circular shape, thinner lemon yellow embroidery and without a ring in the sun, which is embroidered in horizontal stripes, thin black gauze to reverse (diameter: 52 mm).*
69f *Theatre or American made, gold bullion embroidery on thick dark blue wool, thick black gauze to reverse (80 mm x 85 mm). Note that for this division, as is the case with many others that served in both world wars, as well as the Korean War, it is very difficult to positively date such patches. This type of manufacture could well be French from 1918-19, Philippine or Japanese from 1945-46, or even Japanese or Korean from 1950-55. From the 1940s onwards, the patch has been worn in the shape of a diamond with the tip at the top and no longer square-shaped.*
69g *Standard WW2 manufacture, fully embroidered, embroidered in vertical waves on a blue background (60 x 60 mm).*
69h *Variation, without ring at the centre of the sun (63 x 63 mm).*
69i *Variation, enhanced with gold bullion with thick white reinforcing gauze at the reverse of the bullion embroidery (58 x 58 mm).*
69j *WW2 manufacture with olive drab border, without ring, white back, diamond shape (92 x 92 mm, width: 84 mm).*
69k *Variation, embroidered yellow gold sun (96 mm x 96 mm).*
69l *Variation, embroidery known as 'German' type (95 x 92 mm).*
69m *Theatre made, probably Philippine, gilt thread embroidery on royal blue background, reinforced on reverse with black linen backed paper, merrowed blue border around border (88 mm x 88 mm).*

70 - 41st Infantry Division

AC: activated 18 July 1919 in the National Guard under the name of 41st Division. Organized 18 September 1917 at Camp Greene (North Carolina). Inactivated 22 February 1919 at Camp Dix (New Jersey). Reorganized 3 January 1930 in Portland (Oregon) in the Idaho, Montana, Oregon, Washington State and Wyoming National Guard. Federalized 16 September 1940. Reorganized and re-designated 17 February 1942 as the 41st Infantry Division. Inactivated 31 December 1945 in Japan.

A: 28 December 1918 by the AEF.

S: setting sun over the Pacific Ocean, as can be seen in the Northwestern states, whence the unit's recruits came in 1917. Nicknames: 'The Sunset Division, The Jungleers Division.'

C: 14 – 15▲ - 20s.

70a *1925-30 manufacture, red and yellow felt on thick tan twill; the three elements are edged, a horizontal black stripe separates the sun (with 8 sunbeams) from the ocean, thin white gauze to reverse. The red number 10 at the centre of the sun remains a mystery.*
70b *Variation, three pieces of felt sewn onto an olive drab wool background, 12 sunbeams.*
70c *Variation, rougher manufacture, 8 sunbeams.*
70d *1930-40 manufacture, curved embroidery on black wool background, 11 sunbeams.*
70e *Variation, standard embroidery.*
70f *Standard WW2 manufacture with olive drab border, sun with 12 sunbeams.*
70g *Variation, horizontal sun embroidery.*
70h *American WW2 manufacture, even though it has a merrowed edge, this patch is indeed of Second World War vintage. Note the khaki colour of the border.*

Below.
M-1944 wool field jacket for a corporal with the 174th Field Artillery Battalion (155 mm self-propelled guns), a unit belonging to VIIII Corps.
(Author's collection)

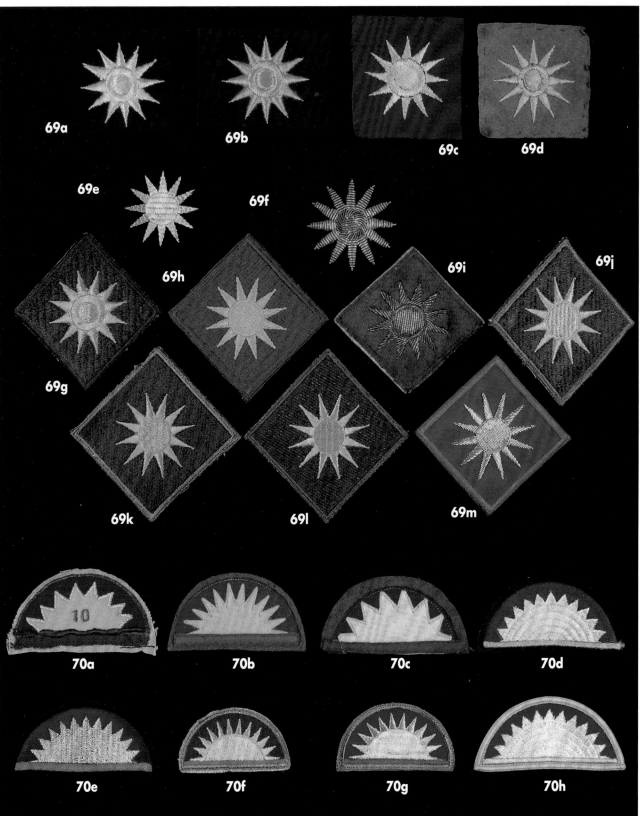

69a

69b

69c

69d

69e

69f

69h

69i

69j

69g

69k

69l

69m

70a

70b

70c

70d

70e

70f

70g

70h

(Florida, other sources cite Hartford in Connecticut). Reorganized and re-designated 43rd Infantry Division 19 February 1942. Inactivated 1 November 1946 at Camp Stoneman (California).

A: 15 March 1923.

S: the four intertwined circles and vine leaf are for the four New England states. The red background signifies that this part of America had been under British rule for many years. Nickname: 'Winged Victory Division,' in honor of its commander, Major-General Leonard F. Wing, the only National Guard general officer to lead a division during WW2. "REDWING"?

C: 11 – 14▲ - 15 – 16.

72a *1930-35 manufacture, probably worn more during WW2. There also exists an embroidered patch on red felt, the number at the centre is embroidered in sky blue, the traditional infantry colour.*
72b *1935-40 manufacture, smaller size, embroidered on red felt, the number was deleted in 1940.*
72c *1940-42 manufacture, embroidered on olive drab wool, the number is no longer present.*
72d *Standard WW2 manufacture, the leaf is well centred, the tips touch the olive drab border.*
72e *Variation, unusual shape and small size.*
72f *Variation. The shape and size of the leaf vary from one manufacture to another.*
72g *Variation.*
72h *Variation, khaki border.*
72i *Variation, green border and back.*

73 - 44th Infantry Division

AC: activated in March 1923 in the National Guard (New York and New Jersey), under the name of 44th Division. Called up for federal service on 16 September 1940 in Trenton (New Jersey). Reorganized and re-designated 44th Infantry Division 16 January 1942. Inactivated 30 November 1945 at Camp Chaffee (Arkansas).

A: 6 October 1921, a year and a half before it was officially organized!

S: the back-to-back number fours are for the numeric designation. The blue and orange colours (yellow in fact) are those of the House of Nassau (Holland) that colonized the region of New York and New Jersey.

Motto: 'Prepared in all things.'

C: 26 - 32 – 34.

73a *1920-25 manufacture, blue and yellow felt.*
73b *1925-40 manufacture, blue embroidery on yellow wool, all sewn onto an olive drab wool background.*
73c *Variation, embroidered on olive drab wool, orange-yellow background.*
73d *Standard WW2 manufacture, olive drab border.*
73e *Variation, orange-yellow background, olive drab border.*
73f *Variation, yellow background.*
73g *Variation, lemon yellow background.*
73h *WW2 manufacture with dark blue merrowed edge. Like the previously seen 41st Division patch (70h), the one here is part of the small series of patches of this type made during WW2.*
73i *Variation, gold bullion background; it is difficult to say if this embroidery was added to a 73h type patch or whether it was originally made in this way.*

71 - 42nd Infantry Division

AC: activated 14 August 1917 in the National Guard under the name of 42nd Infantry Division. Organized at Camp Mills (New York) 5 September 1917. Inactivated 9 May 1919 at Camp Dix (New Jersey). Reorganized 5 February 1943, under the name of 42nd Infantry Division. Organized 14 July 1943 at Camp Gruber (Oklahoma). Inactivated 29 June 1946 in Austria.

A: 29 October 1918 by the AEF, modified in July 1943 by the addition of an olive green border.

S: the rainbow signifies that during the Great War, the men that made up the division came from 26 states. Also present is the infantry blue, cavalry yellow and red of the artillery. Nickname: 'Rainbow Division.'

C: 25-26-34.

71a *Standard WW2 manufacture, embroidery in curved stripes.*
71b *Variation, standard embroidery.*
71c *Variation, lemon yellow.*
71d *Insignia painted on leather, probably for the leather jacket of an artillery observation or liaison pilot.*

72 - 43rd Infantry Division

AC: activated 21 March 1923 in the National Guard (Connecticut-Maine-Rhode Island-Vermont) as the 43rd Division. Called up for federal service on 24 February 1941 at Camp Blanding

Top left.
A 43rd Division corporal in the USA at the beginning of the war. The distinctive insignia on the lapels are those of the 172nd Infantry (Vermont National Guard).
(Coleman collection)

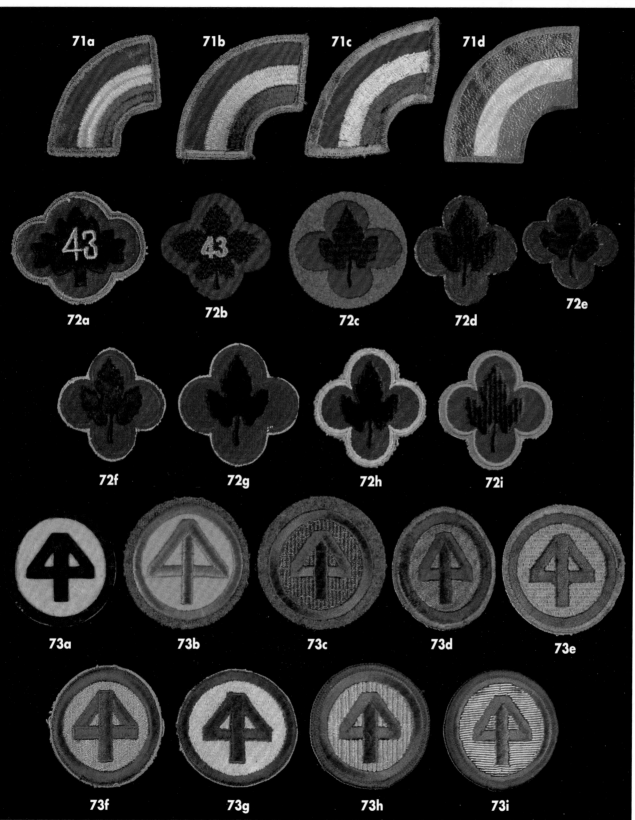

71a 71b 71c 71d

72a 72b 72c 72d 72e

72f 72g 72h 72i

73a 73b 73c 73d 73e

73f 73g 73h 73i

55

KNOW YOUR INSIGNIA.

For many years, the shoulder patch of the 45th Division was a Swastika, a good luck symbol of its personnel. When Adolph Hitler Division originally drew much of the Indian Country from which the proclaimed the Swastika as the sign of the National Socialist Party in Germany, the Division abandoned it. That was one of the first things Hitler fouled up for us.

The Thunderbird, too, is a symbol from the Indian Country. As a matter of historical fact, most tribes from the Arctic Circle to Panama have used it in their crude painting and weaving. It was the "giver of rain" and, as such, was highly regarded by the Indians of the American Southwest. The Thunderbird was a gigantic creature who, according to Indian lore, not only brought the rain but also provided the thunder and lightning that accompanied it.

The method of producing these phenomena was simply. The lightning emanated from his piercing eyes, the thunder was caused by the flapping of the giant creature's tremendous wings, and the rain was a portable affair, being carried in the form of a lake on the great bird's back! When the bird was favorably inclined toward a certain territory, it would go into a wingover and the valleys below became fertile and green with abundant moisture.

Because rain was so essential to the dry southwest, the Thunderbird became a symbol of good luck and, because of its tremendous size and its capability of creating thunder and lightning, it was regarded with awe. It was wise to placate the Thunderbird since it could either prevent the fall of rain entirely or drop so much of it as to cause floods as destruction. (It is not official, of course, but wherever the Thunderbird patch has gone-Sicily, Italy, France and Germany-there has been nothing mythical about the "very unusual weather" that accompanied it. Any G. I. will vouch for that.)

The golden Thunderbird, set against the background of a red patch, is now part of the proud tradition of the 45th Division, and is a familiar insignia to friend and foe alike. Its military reputation, now almost legendary, has been earned by the blood, sweat and courage of fighting men of the 45th.

Far left.
2nd Lieutenant Van T. Barfoot of the 157th Infantry, 45th Division was awarded the Medal of Honor by General Patch on 28 September 1944 in Epinal. The divisional patch, on the left shoulder of the shirt, appears to be the type with olive drab border.
(National Archives)

Left.
This letter, handed out to the division's recruits, explains the reasons why the emblem was chosen for the 45th; it bears a stapled second type patch. This was a fairly unusual initiative by a unit commander.

74e *Standard WW2 manufacture, green edge and back (65 x 65 mm).*
74f *Variation, white back, diamond shape.*
74g *Variation, lemon yellow Thunderbird.*
74h *Variation, horizontal type embroidery.*
74i *Variation, diamond shape.*
74j *Variation, diagonal embroidery on red background and horizontal for the bird.*
74k *WW2 manufacture, woven with motif in negative on back, known as 'Italian theatre made.*
74l *German or Austrian made; bright gold bullion highlighted with black.*
74m *European theatre made, WW2, gold bullion on red felt background.*

74 - 45th Infantry Division

AC: activated 19 October 1920 in the National Guard as the 45th Division. Organized 3 August 1923 in Oklahoma City. Called up for federal service 16 September 1940 from Arizona, Colorado, New Mexico and Oklahoma National Guard units. Re-designated 45th Infantry Division 23 February 1942. Inactivated 7 December 1945 at Camp Bowie (Texas).
A: first type: exact date unknown, worn from 1924 to 1939; second type: 22 May 1939.
S: first type, yellow swastika on red background, an ancient Indian symbol of luck. It was decided to change the emblem as it was now associated with the nazi regime in Germany. A different Indian symbol for luck was chosen for the second type: the Thunderbird. The colours are those of the Kingdom of Spain, the former colonial power of the regions where the unit's men came from at its creation. The four sides of the square symbolize Arizona, Colorado, New Mexico and Oklahoma. Nickname: 'The Thunderbird Division'. Motto: "Semper Anticus" ("Always Forward").
C: 24 – 25 – 26 – 29▲ - 34 – 35 – 36s - 37s.

74a *First type, two pieces of sewn felt.*
74b *Embroidered on thick red twill, overstitched border, thin white gauze to reverse.*
74c *Embroidered on red wool, thin border around swastika, thin white gauze on back.*
74d *Second type, 1939-42, embroidered on olive drab wool, thin white gauze to reverse.*

75 - 63rd Infantry Division

AC: activated 18 January 1943. Organized 15 June 1943 at Camp Blanding (Florida). Inactivated 27 September 1945 at Camp Myles Standish (Massachusetts).
A: 27 March 1943.
S: the sword of justice upon the flames of hell, a reminder of Winston Churchill's quote: "The enemy will bleed and burn in expiation for their crimes against humanity" (Casablanca Conference, January 1943). This graphic quote led to the unit's nickname of 'Blood and Fire Division'.
C: 26 – 34.

75a *Standard WW2 manufacture, golden yellow sword, plain grip (53 x 80 mm).*
75b *Variation, thin border around the flames, detailed sword grip.*
75c *Variation, lemon yellow sword with detailed grip.*
75d *Variation, thin border around the sword.*
75e *WW2 European made, probably German, red cotton thread and gold bullion on olive drab wool, black paper glued to reverse.*
There is also a patch with silver sword (gray) on a dark brown background. Another type with a very thin yellow border is known, probably made between 1950-60 and specific to the Division's reconnaissance unit, yellow being the traditional colour of the cavalry.

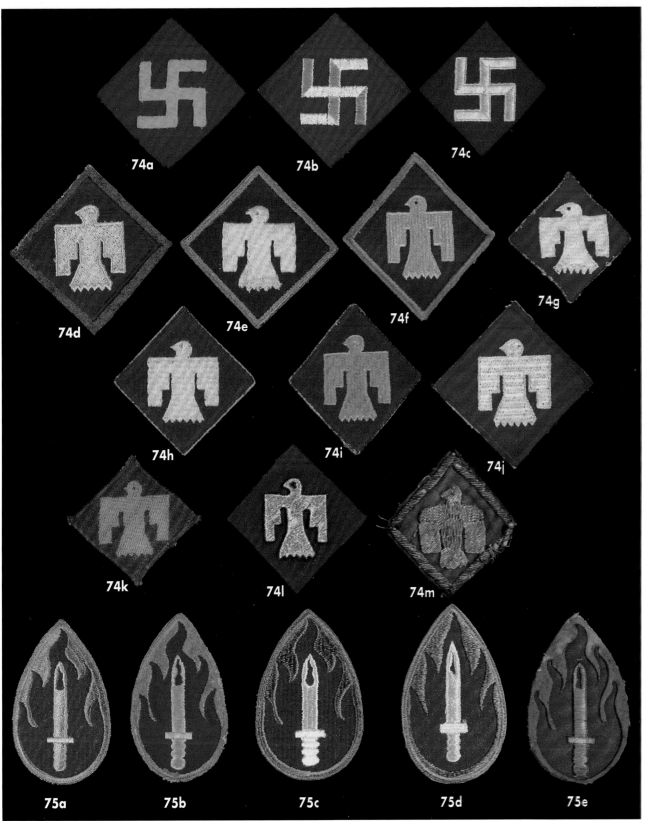

74a

74b

74c

74d

74e

74f

74g

74h

74i

74j

74k

74l

74m

75a

75b

75c

75d

75e

 77a *First type, standard manufacture from April to August 1943, lemon yellow background, yellow panther mouth, no whiskers (diameter 62 mm).*
77b *Variation, golden yellow background.*
77c *Variation, red mouth.*
77d *Variation, with whiskers.*
77e *Second type, standard manufacture starting from August 1943 (diameter 68 mm).*
77f *Variation, differences in the eyes (numerous variations can be seen according to manufacturers).*
77g *Variation, lemon yellow background, ear outlined in white.*
77h *European made, woven yellow background, embroidered head and edge, black paper glued to reverse.*

78 - 69th Infantry Division

AC: activated 14 January 1943. Organized 15 May 1943 at Camp Shelby (Mississippi). Inactivated 18 September 1945 at Camp Kilmer (New Jersey).
A: 30 April 1943.
S: the figures 6 and 9 head to tail for the numeric designation, in the national colours. Designed by the division's first commander, Major General CL Bolte. Nickname: 'The Fighting 69th'.
C: 28 – 34.

78a *Standard WW2 manufacture (55 x 68 mm).*
78b *Variation, the corners are more rounded, the separation between the blue and red numbers is narrower.*
78c *Variation, white borders are thinner.*

79 - 70th Infantry Division

AC: activated 18 January 1943. Organized 16 June 1943 at Camp Adair (Oregon). Inactivated 11 October 1945 at Camp Kilmer (New Jersey).
A: 15 June 1943.
S: the axe symbolizes the will to drive through obstacles. The mountain is a reminder of Mount Hood which was not far from the area where the unit was formed. The pine tree evokes the training area as well as the 91st Division (see page 71). The red background symbolizes the blood shed by the founders of Oregon. Nickname: 'The Trailblazer Division'.
C: 25-26-34.

79a *Standard WW2 manufacture (55 x 68 mm).*
79b *Variation, vertical embroidery for the axe, lighter green pine tree (numerous shades of green can be seen; the same applies to the shape of the tree and the mountain).*
79c *Variation, 'German' type embroidery.*
79d *European made, bullion and cotton (pine tree) embroidery on a red wool background, thick reinforcing twill to reverse.*

Top left.
Outside the St. Nazaire pocket (Western France), in March 1945, this artilleryman from the 871st FAB prepares a 105-mm shell. The 66th Division patch is sewn to his shirt sleeve.
(National Archives)

76 - 65th Infantry Division

AC: activated 12 March 1943. Organized 16 August 1943 at Camp Shelby (Mississippi). Inactivated 31 August 1945 in Austria.
A: 25 May 1943.
S: white battle axe on a blue background, the traditional colours of the infantry; Nickname: 'The Battle axe Division'.
C: 26 – 34.

76a *Standard WW2 manufacture (52 x 68 mm).*
76b *Variation, slightly different axe (there are numerous variations), the shield is more rounded at the top.*

77 - 66th Infantry Division

AC: activated 16 December 1942. Organized 15 April 1943 at Camp Blanding (Florida). Inactivated 8 November 1945 at Camp Kilmer (New Jersey).
A: first type: 13 April 1943; second type: 26 August 1943.
S: first type, leaping black panther symbolizing ferocity in attack. For an unknown reason, this type, according to the commander of the division Major General Kramer, might make those wearing it the subject of jibes, therefore it was replaced by a new design in August 1943.
Second type: black roaring panther head with the same symbolism as before. Nickname: 'The Black Panther Division'.
C: 32.

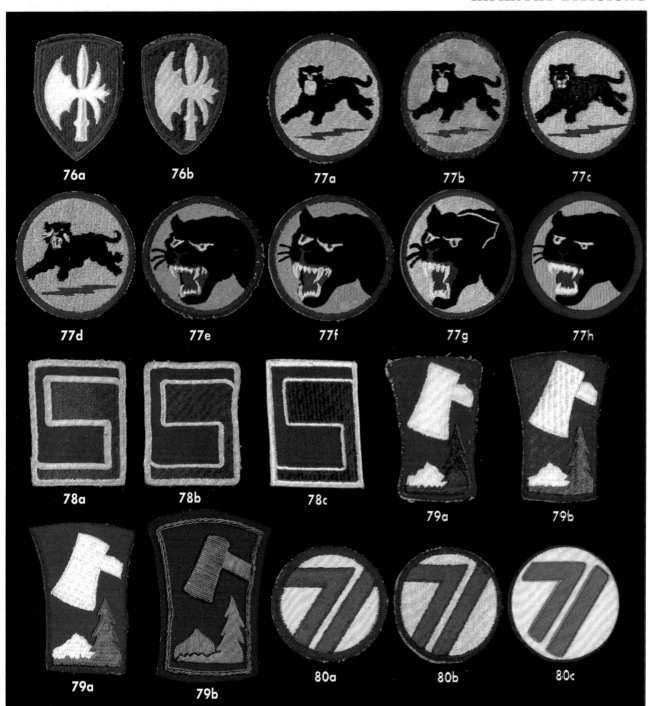

76a   76b   77a   77b   77c

77d   77e   77f   77g   77'h

78a   78b   78c   79a   79b

79a   79b   80a   80b   80c

80 - 71st Infantry Division

AC: activated 10 July 1943, under the name of 71st Light Division, Pack-Jungle. Organized 15 July 1943 at Camp Carson (Colorado). Re-designated 71st Infantry Division 26 May 1944. Inactivated 11 March 1946 at Camp Kilmer (New Jersey).
A: 24 July 1944.

S: numbers Seven and One for the numeric designation with the three national colours. Nickname (unofficial): 'The Red Circle Division'.
C: 26 – 34.

80a *WW2 manufacture, embroidered on white twill.*
80b *Standard WW2 manufacture, fully embroidered (diameter 62 mm).*
80c *WW2 European made, blue cotton and gold bullion, red silk used for the border, white paper to reverse.*

81 - 75th Infantry Division

AC: activated 24 December 1942. Organized 15 April 1943 at Fort Leonard Wood (Missouri). Inactivated 14 November 1945 at Camp Patrick Henry (Virginia).
A: 12 February 1943.
S: numbers Seven and Five for the numeric designation and the national colours.
C: 25 – 26 – 34

81a *Standard WW2 manufacture (62 x 68 mm).*
81b *Variation, thin border to the white stripe.*
81c *WW2 European manufacture in blue, white and red wool sewn onto olive drab wool, silver bullion outlines, reinforcing twill glued to reverse.*

82 - 76th Infantry Division

AC: activated 5 August 1917 under the name of 76th Division, organized 26 August 1917 at Camp Devens (Massachusetts), inactivated 14 January 1919 at the same location. Assigned 24 June 1921 to the Organized Reserve. Activated 16 June 1942 and reorganized at Fort George G. Meade (Maryland). Re-designated as 76th Infantry Division 1 August 1942, then as Replacement Pool Division from 2 October 1942 to 1 March 1943, the date upon which it took back its previous designation. Inactivated 31 August 1945 in Germany.
A: 14 March 1919 by the AEF.
S: the white 'label' is a heraldic symbol of cadency, as the division was the first to be formed with National Army conscripts during the Great War. Nickname: 'Onaway Division.'
C: 25 – 26 – 34.

82a *Standard WW2 manufacture, khaki edge, black back (65 x 62 mm).*
82b *Variation, white back.*
82c *Variation, white back, olive drab border.*
82d *Variation, vertical type blue and red embroidery.*
82e *Variation, 'German' type embroidery.*
82f *Variation, separation strip between the blue and red embroidered in white, like the 1919 patch.*
82g *WW2 European manufacture, blue and red felt sewn onto white twill, border and 'label' in silver bullion.*

83 - 77th Infantry Division

AC: activated 5 August 1917, organized 18 August 1917 under the name of 77th Division at Camp Upton (New York), inactivated 9 May 1919 at the same location. Assigned 24 June 1921 to the Organized Reserve. Activated 25 March 1942 and reorganized at Fort Jackson (South Carolina), re-designated 77th Infantry Division 1 August 1942. Inactivated 15 March 1946 in Japan.
A: 23 October 1918 by the AEF.
S: the Statue of Liberty lighting up the World symbolizes New York, the area from which the men originated in WW1. Nickname: 'Statue of Liberty Division.'
C: 13▲ - 19▲ - 21.

83a *Standard WW2 manufacture, dark blue background, golden yellow detailed statue (50 x 68 mm), the American made non-regulation 'Okinawa' tab was worn by veterans of said campaign.*
83b *Variation, lemon yellow statue.*
83c *Variation, light blue background, golden yellow statue.*
83d *As with the previous patch, green back, slightly different statue.*
83e *Theatre made, probably Japanese, blue felt sewn onto a khaki background glued to stock, gold bullion embroidery, thin black-dyed silk to reverse.*

84 - 78th Infantry Division

AC: activated 5 August 1917 under the name of 78th Division, organized 22 August 1917 at Camp Dix (New Jersey), inactivated 9 July 1919 at the same location. Assigned 24 June 1921 to the Organized Reserve. Activated and reorganized at Fort Butner (North Carolina) as the 78th Infantry Division, 15 August 1942. Replacement Pool Division from 2 October 1942 to 1 March 1943, then reverted to its previous designation. Inactivated 22 May 1946 in Germany.
A: 19 October 1918 by the AEF. The lightning bolt was added on 24 January 1919.
S: initially a straightforward olive drab, then red, semi-circle. The white bolt of lightning is a reminder of the citation received from the French command in 1918: "(This division is) a bolt of lightning that leaves the battlefield red with the blood of the enemy". Nickname: 'The Lightning Division,' motto: "Audaciter" (Boldness).
C: 25 – 26 – 34.

84a *1925-30 manufacture, embroidered on red wool, thin white gauze to back.*
84b *Standard WW2 manufacture (80 x 45 mm).*
84c *Variation, olive drab border and back.*
84s *Variation, white back.*
84e *Variation, khaki edge.*
84f *Variation, olive drab edge, thinner lightning bolt.*
84g *WW2 European made, thin red material with tan twill backing.*
84h *German made 1945-46, the silver bullion is typical, thick black reinforcing twill to reverse.*

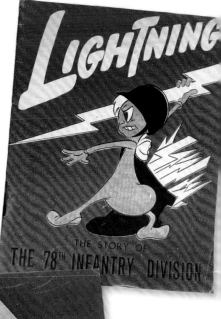

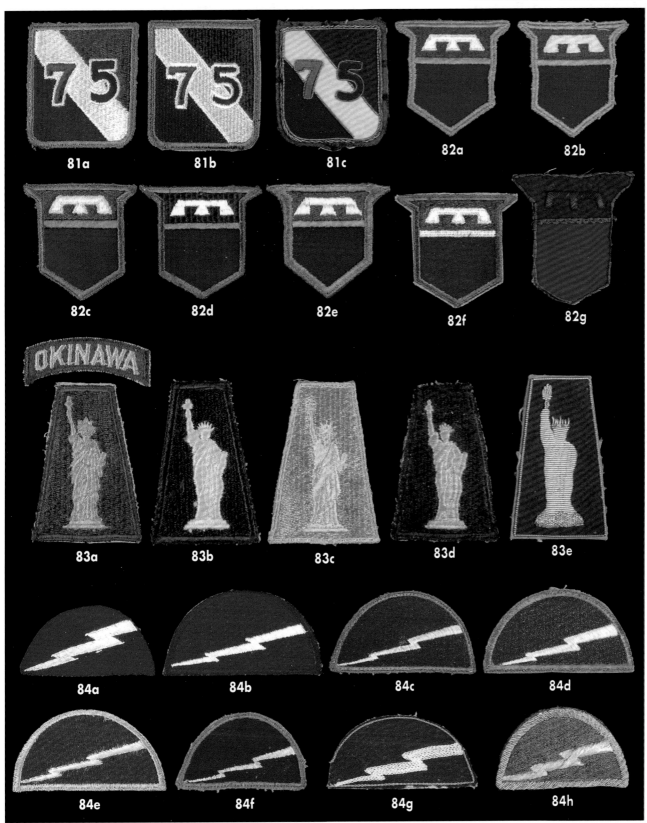

81a

81b

81c

82a

82b

82c

82d

82e

82f

82g

OKINAWA

83a

83b

83c

83d

83e

84a

84b

84c

84d

84e

84f

84g

84h

85 - 79th Infantry Division

AC: activated 5 August 1917 under the name of 79th Division. Organized at Camp Meade (Maryland) 25 August 1917. Inactivated 2 June 1919 at Camp Dix (New Jersey). Assigned 24 June 1921 to the Organized Reserve. Activated 15 June 1942, reorganized at Camp Pickett (Virginia) and re-designated 73th Infantry Division 1 August 1942. Inactivated 11 December 1945 at Camp Kilmer (New Jersey).

A: 15 November 1918 by the AEF.

S: the Cross of Lorraine is a reminder of the division's participation in the fighting in Eastern France during the Great War. Initially white, the cross became gray in the years 1935-40 to symbolize the joining of southern and northern states.
Nickname: 'Cross of Lorraine Division.'

C: 15 – 26 – 30 – 32 – 34.

85a *Standard WW2 manufacture, white cross and border, colour identical to the patch approved during WW1 (50 x 60 mm).*
85b *Very thin background twill and embroidery thread, black back. According to some American authors, this is British made but this seems extremely doubtful. On the other hand, it could be French as many 1944-45 French Army badges are similar.*
85c *Standard WW2 manufacture, gray cross and border. The change in colour was made official in 1935 but was not seen on patches until later, note the double blue border.*
85d *Variation.*
85e *Variation, thinner cross and border.*
85f *Variation, vertical embroidery.*
85g *Comparable to 85b, white back.*
85h *Standard patch enhanced with silver bullion, white reinforcing gauze to reverse.*
85i *1945 German manufacture, dark blue background, typical silver bullion (compare with 85h), a thin, darker bullion edge surrounds the border, black paper to reverse.*
85j *Tailor made, silver bullion on dark blue wool, thick white twill to reverse.*

86 - 80th Infantry Division

AC: activated 5 August 1917 as 80th Division. Organized at Camp Lee (Virginia) 27 August 1917, inactivated 5 June 1919 at the same place. Assigned 24 June 1921 within the Organized Reserve, organized in December 1921 in Richmond (Virginia). Activated 15 July 1942, reorganized at Camp Forrest (Tennessee) and re-designated 80th Infantry Division 1 August 1942. Inactivated 4 January 1946 at Camp Kilmer (New Jersey).

A: 20 October 1918 by the AEF.

S: the three mountains symbolize the states of Pennsylvania, Virginia and West Virginia where the division's men came from in 1917. Nickname: 'Blue Ridge Division.' Motto: "The 80th Only Moves Forward."

C: 25 – 26 – 32 – 34.

86a *Standard WW2 manufacture, non-spec. dark blue mountains, although this was chosen when the patch was approved in 1918. Vertical background embroidery (55 x 58 mm).*
86b *European made on shirt material, reinforced on reverse with dark gray twill, chain stitch embroidery.*
86c *European made, olive drab wool background (which could be blanket cloth), cotton embroidery, thin white gauze backing.*
86d *Standard WW2 manufacture, sky blue mountains (regulation colour), khaki detailing on the mountains (which can also be seen on patches with dark blue mountains).*
86e *Standard WW2 manufacture, vertical embroidery.*

87 - 81st Infantry Division

AC: activated 5 August 1917 as 81st Division. Organized 25 August 1917 at Camp Jackson (South Carolina). Inactivated 11 June 1919 at Hoboken (New Jersey). Assigned 24 June 1921 to the Organized Reserve. Activated 15 June 1942, reorganized at Camp Rucker (Alabama) and re-designated 81st Infantry Division 1 August 1942. Inactivated 20 January 1946 in Japan.

A: 19 October 1918 by the AEF.

S: the black cat as a reminder that the division trained near Wildcat Creek in 1917. The 81st was the first division to wear a distinctive patch, well before they were authorized and its arrival in France (see page 4). Nickname: 'The Wildcat Division.' Motto: "Wildcats Never Quit. They Win or Die."

C: 13 – 21.

87a *1925-35 manufacture, embroidered on olive drab wool.*
87b *Standard WW2 manufacture (diameter 55 mm).*
87c *Variation, thin outline around the cat. There are a great variety of shapes concerning the cat, depending on manufacturers.*
87d *Variation, vertical embroidery (diameter 57 mm).*
87e *Variation, olive drab border (diameter 58 mm).*

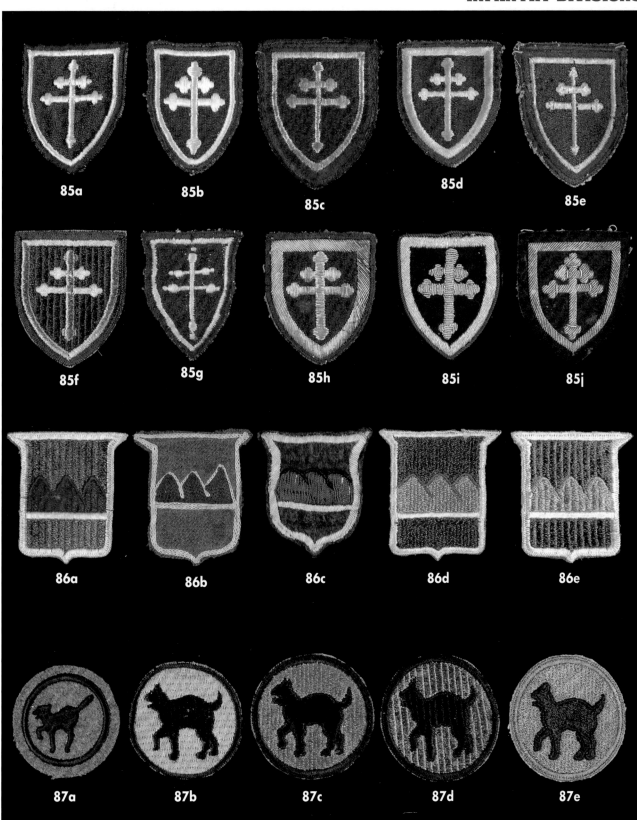

85a

85b

85c

85d

85e

85f

85g

85h

85i

85j

86a

86b

86c

86d

86e

87a

87b

87c

87d

87e

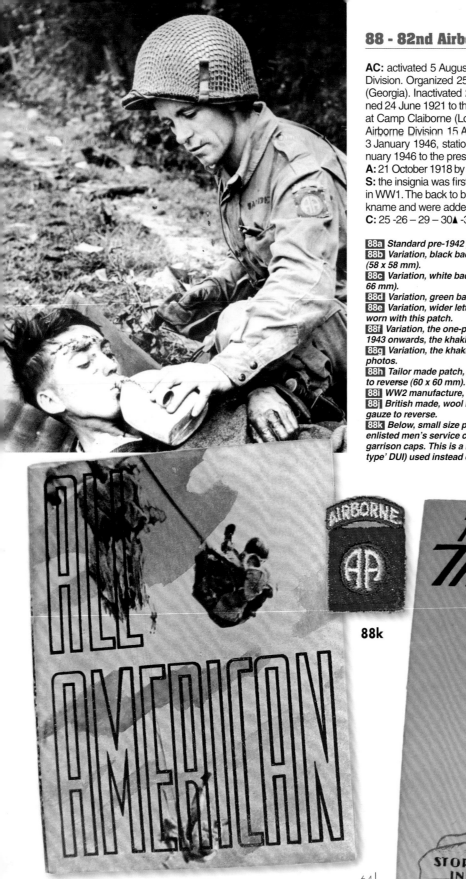

88 - 82nd Airborne Division

AC: activated 5 August 1917 under the name of 82nd Division. Organized 25 August 1917 at Camp Gordon (Georgia). Inactivated 27 May 1918 at Camp Mills (New York). Assigned 24 June 1921 to the Organized Reserve. Activated 25 March 1942 at Camp Claiborne (Louisiana). Reorganized and re-designated 82nd Airborne Division 15 August 1942. Returned to the United States on 3 January 1946, stationed at Fort Bragg (North Carolina) from 16 January 1946 to the present day.

A: 21 October 1918 by the AEF. 'Airborne' tab added on 31 August 1942.

S: the insignia was first painted on the division's vehicles and baggage in WW1. The back to back initials A are the division's 'All American' nickname and were added when the divisional patch was chosen.

C: 25 -26 – 29 – 30▲ -36 – 34▲.

88a *Standard pre-1942 patch (55 x 58 mm).*
88b *Variation, black back, the separate tab also has a black back (58 x 58 mm).*
88c *Variation, white back, larger dimensions and matching tab (63 66 mm).*
88d *Variation, green back.*
88e *Variation, wider letters, mismatched tab, but nevertheless the one worn with this patch.*
88f *Variation, the one-piece patch and tab appeared from approximately 1943 onwards, the khaki twill background remains visible between them.*
88g *Variation, the khaki twill had been cut out, as is often seen in period photos.*
88h *Tailor made patch, probably American, felt background, black paper to reverse (60 x 60 mm).*
88i *WW2 manufacture, 'German' type embroidery.*
88j *British made, wool background, white cotton embroidery, thin white gauze to reverse.*
88k *Below, small size patch (27 x 34 mm) designed to be worn on the enlisted men's service coat lapels, officer's coats shoulder straps, and garrison caps. This is a non-regulation Distinguishing Unit Insignia ('Patch type' DUI) used instead of an identical enamelled badge.*

88k

88a 88b 88c 88d 88e

88f 88g 88h 88i 88j

89 - 83rd Infantry Division

AC: activated 5 August 1917 as the 83rd Division, organized 25 August 1917 at Camp Sherman (Ohio) and inactivated 8 October 1919 in the same location. Assigned 24 June 1921 to the Organized Reserve. Activated 15 August 1942, reorganized at Camp Atterbury (Indiana) and re-designated 83rd Infantry Division. Inactivated 27 March 1946 at Camp Kilmer (New Jersey).

A: 26 December 1918 by the AEF.

S: the four superposed OHIO initials are a reminder of where the

division trained in 1917.

C: 25 – 26 – 30 – 32 – 34.

89a *Standard WW2 manufacture (62 x 61 mm).*
89b *Variation, 'German' type black background embroidery, very thin letters.*
89c *Variation.*
89d *Variation*
89e *Variation, olive drab border, vertical embroidery.*
89f *Variation, white (?) embroidered design .*
89g *European manufacture, gold bullion embroidered letters on a thin wool background, thin twill to reverse.*

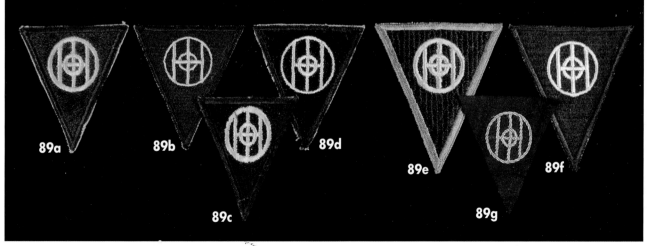

89a 89b 89c 89d 89e 89f 89g

83rd Division

90 - 84th Infantry Division

AC: activated 5 August 1917 under the name of 84th Division, organized 25 August 1917 at Camp Zachary Taylor (Kentucky) and inactivated 25 July 1919 at the same place. Assigned 26 June 1921 to the Organized Reserve. Activated 15 October 1942, reorganized at Camp Howze (Texas) and re-designated 84th Infantry Division. Inactivated 21 January 1946 at Camp Kilmer (New Jersey).
A: April 1919 by the AEF, confirmed 16 February 1924.
S: the axe and split rail symbolize the men who built railway lines, like president Abraham Lincoln did to fund his law studies (the 84th Division bore his name in 1917-19). Nickname: "The Railsplitters'.
C: 25 – 26 – 34.

90a *Standard WW2 manufacture, green back (diameter 65 mm).*
90b *Variation, white back. The German made 'Railsplitters' tab' dates from 1945 (as seen on a shirt sleeve, bottom right): white embroidery on red twill, gray reinforcing cloth to reverse.*
90c *Variation.*
90d *German manufacture, silver bullion and green cotton border on a red wool background, rigidified by black paper glued to the reverse.*

91 - 85th Infantry Division

AC: activated 5 August 1917 as 85th Division, organized 25 August 1917 at Camp Custer (Michigan). Inactivated 18 April 1919 at the same location. Assigned 24 June 1921 to the Organized Reserve. Activated 15 May 1942 and reorganized at Camp Shelby (Mississippi). Re-designated 85th Infantry Division 1 August 1942. Inactivated 25 August 1945 at Camp Patrick Henry (Virginia).
A: 24 December 1918 by the AEF.
S: the C and D initials of the nickname 'Custer Division,' a reminder of where the unit trained in 1917.
C: 31 – 33 – 35.

91a *Standard WW2 manufacture (diameter 54 mm).*
91b *Variation (diameter 58 mm).*
91c *Variation (diameter 55 mm).*
91d *Variation, green back (diameter 60 mm).*
91e *Variation, white back (diameter 65 mm).*

92 - 86th Infantry Division

AC: activated 5 August 1917 under the name of 80th Division, organized 25 August 1917 at Camp Grant (Illinois), inactivated in January 1919 at the same place. Assigned 24 June 1921 to the Organized Reserve. Activated, reorganized and re-designated 80th Infantry Division 15 December 1942 at Camp Howze (Texas). Inactivated 30 December 1946 in the Philippines.
A: 25 November 1918 by the AEF.
S: black hawk and letters B and H for the unit's nickname: 'The Blackhawk Division.'

92a *1925-35 manufacture, embroidery on red wool, thin white gauze to reverse (70 x 90 mm).*
92b *Standard WW2 manufacture, green back (58 x 63 mm).*
92c *White back, variation in the shape of the hawk (a great many variations in the shape of hawk and letters can be seen depending on manufacturers).*
92d *Variation (55 x 62 mm).*
92e *Variation (82 x 88 mm).*

93 - 87th Infantry Division

AC: activated 5 August 1917 under the name of 87th Division, organized 25 August 1917 at Camp Pike (Arkansas), inactivated 14 February 1919 at the same place. Assigned 24 June 1921 to the Organized Reserve. Activated 15 December 1942 and reorganized at Camp McCain (Mississippi) as the 87th Infantry Division. Inactivated 21 September 1945 at Fort Benning (Georgia).
A: 9 November 1918 by the AEF.
S: the yellow acorn, the traditional symbol of strength, also the unit's nickname: 'Golden Acorn Division.' Motto: "Stalwart and Strong, and sturdy as an oak."
C: 25 – 26 – 34.

93a *Standard WW2 manufacture, mid green background, lemon yellow acorn (many colour variations exist from one manufacturer to another) diameter 55 mm.*
93b *Variation, green back (diameter 55 mm).*
93c *Variation, white back (diameter 56 mm).*
93d *Variation, very pale colours, khaki border, black back. Identified by some American authors as British manufacture (diameter 53 mm).*
93e *European made, green wool background, gold bullion embroidery and border, backed with white twill (diameter 61 mm).*
93f *European made, probably German, green wool background, gold bullion embroidery, green cotton inner border, thick white reinforcing twill to reverse (diameter 60 mm).*

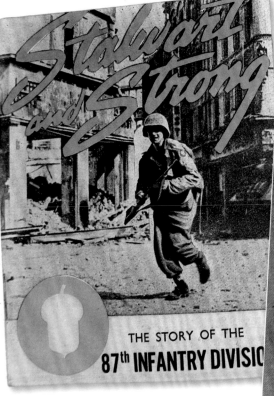

THE STORY OF THE
87th INFANTRY DIVISIO[N]

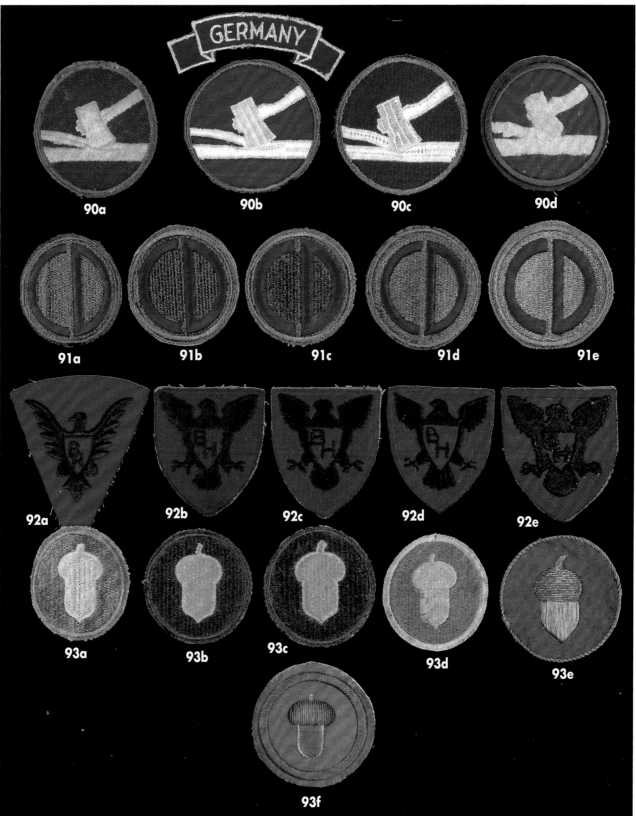

GERMANY

90a 90b 90c 90d

91a 91b 91c 91d 91e

92a 92b 92c 92d 92e

93a 93b 93c 93d 93e

93f

Sewn on a shirt, a standard WW2 patch for the 88th Division and an Italian made scroll. Many similar scrolls exist for the division's components, embroidered in cotton thread or bullion. These are typical of the 88th Division, and more generally of Italian theatre units.
(Author's collection)

Left.
This picture taken in an Italian studio shows a Pfc of the 88th Division, whose shoulder patch is visible on the M-1944 wool field jacket's left sleeve. The unit insignia on the lapels are for the 349th Infantry.
(Coleman collection)

Below.
An enlisted man's flannel shirt with the 44th Infantry Division shoulder patch.
(Author's collection)

94 - 88th Infantry Division

AC: activated 5 August 1917 as the 88th Division, organized 25 August 1917 at Camp Dodge (Iowa) and inactivated 10 June 1919 at the same place. Assigned 24 June 1921 to the Organized Reserve. Activated 15 July 1942, reorganized at Camp Gruber (Oklahoma), re-designated 88th Infantry Division 1 August 1942. Inactivated 24 October 1947 in Italy.

A: 9 November 1918 by the AEF.

S: blue quatrefoil symbolizing luck and the four states from which the division's recruits came in 1917. The leaf also forms two intertwined 8s for the numeric designation; the blue colour is for the infantry. Nicknames: 'The Blue Devil Division/The Cloverleaf Division.'

C: 31 – 33 – 35.

94a *Standard WW2 shoulder patch (55 x 55 mm)*
94a *Variation (62 x 62 mm).*
94c *Variation, olive drab border.*
94d *German or Austrian made 1945-47, woven with khaki reinforcing twill to reverse.*
94e *Italian made WW2, blue twill, white border. Supposedly for Divisional headquarters personnel.*
94f *Variation, red border (artillery), unbacked.*
94g *Variation, silver bullion border, thin white gauze to reverse.*

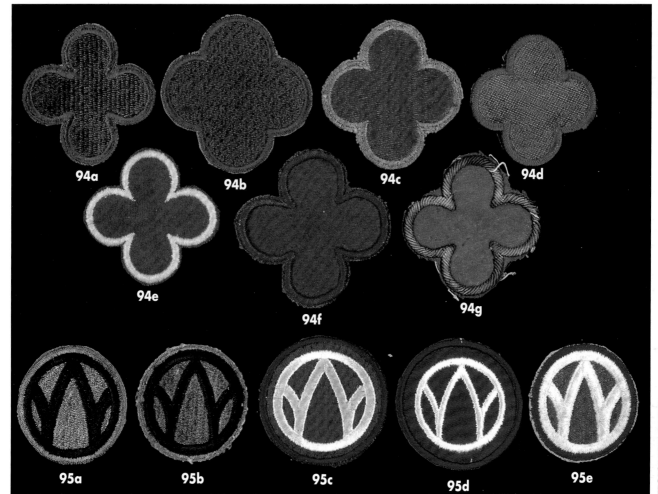

94a 94b 94c 94d

94e 94f 94g

95a 95b 95c 95d 95e

95 - 89th Infantry Division

AC: activated 5 August 1917 under the name of 89th Division, organized 13 August 1917 at Camp Funston (Kansas) and inactivated at the same place 12 June 1919. Assigned 24 June 1921 to the Organized Reserve as HQ, 89th Division.

Re-designated 89th Division 22 February 1942, activated 15 July 1942, reorganized at Camp Carson (Colorado) and re-designated 89th Infantry Division 1 August 1942. Reorganized 1 August 1943 as the 89th Light Division (Truck).

Reverted to 89th Infantry Division on 15 June 1944. Inactivated 17 December 1945 at Camp Shanks (New York).

A: 25 October 1918 by the AEF.

S: the inverted W could be read as an M, being the two initials of the nickname 'Middle West Division,' as the 89th was raised with recruits from the Midwest in 1917.

The tricolour patch variation was seen towards the end of the war and not authorized until December 1948 when the unit was reactivated.

Nicknames: 'The Middle West Division/The Rolling W Division.' Motto: "Get it done."

C: 25 – 26.

95a *First type patch, standard WW2 manufacture (diameter 55 mm).*
95b *Variation, browner background, green back.*
95c *Second type patch in the national colours (non-regulation prior to 1948), early American make (diameter 63 mm).*
95d *Variation, European made, embroidered on blue twill, reinforced to reverse with glued white gauze (diameter 63 mm).*
95e *Standard manufacture, probably made for veterans.*

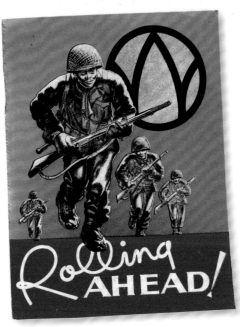

Rolling AHEAD!

96 – 90th Infantry Division

AC: activated 5 August 1917 as 90th Division. Organized 25 August 1917 at Camp Travis (Texas). Inactivated 17 June 1919 at Camp Bowie (Texas). Assigned 24 June 1921 to the Organized Reserve. Activated 25 March 1942 and reorganized at Camp Berkeley (Texas). Re-designated 90th Infantry Division 1 August 1942, reorganized 15 September 1942 as the 90th Motorized Division, reverted to standard infantry division on 19 May 1943. Inactivated 27 December 1945 at Camp Shanks (New York).
A: 25 October 1918 by the AEF.
S: the T and O are initials of the unit's nickname 'Texas & Oklahoma' (states from which the unit's men were levied in WW1), which later became 'Tough Ombres.'
C: 25 – 26 – 30▲ - 32 – 34.

96a *Standard WW2 manufacture (53 x 53 mm).*
96b *Variation.*
96c *Variation, thin red border around the letters.*
96d *Variation.*
96e *Variation, thin red border around the letters.*
96f *Variation, olive green back.*
96g *Variation, embroidery known as German.*
96h *WW2 American manufacture with rounded top. Despite being non-regulation type, it was the shape of the 1918 patch (57 x 57 mm).*

97 - 91st Infantry Division

A: activated 5 August 1917 under the name of 91st Division. Organized 26 August 1917 at Camp Lewis (Washington). Inactivated 13 May 1919 at the Presidio of San Francisco (California). Assigned 24 June 1921 to the Organized Reserve, organized 7 October 1921 in San Francisco (California). Activated 15 August 1942 and reorganized at Camp White (Oregon) as the 91st Infantry Division. Inactivated 11 December 1945 at Camp Rucker (Alabama).
A: 8 December 1918 by the AEF.
S: the pine tree symbolizes Oregon, the home state of the division's men in WW1. Nickname: 'Powder River Division.'
C: 31 – 33 – 35.

97a *Standard WW2 manufacture, dark green (many different shades of green can be seen), jagged edge (regulation type), 50 x 63 mm.*
97b *Variation, light green.*
97c *Variation, green back.*
97d *Variation, straight edge (non regulation), horizontal embroidery.*
97e *Variation 97a, embroidery known as 'German.'*
97f *Variation 97c, olive drab border.*
97g *Variation 97d, standard embroidery, olive drab border.*

98 - 92nd Infantry Division

AC: activated 24 October 1917 under the name of 92nd Division. Organized 29 October 1917 at Camp Funston (Kansas). Inactivated 7 March 1919 at Camp Upton (New York). Reactivated 5 May 1942 as the 92nd Infantry Division. Organized 15 October 1942 at Fort McClellan (Alabama),
deactivated 28 November 1945 at the same place. This was the first infantry division entirely formed with colored personnel, except for field grade officers and generals.
A: 23 October 1918 by the AEF, confirmed 9 December 1918.
S: The black buffalo is a reminder of the 'Buffalo' Soldiers, a name given by Native American Indians during the Indian Wars due to their frizzy hair and also because they often wore buffalo pelts during the winter campaigns. Nickname: 'Buffalo Division.'
C: 31 – 33 – 35.

98a *Standard WW2 patch (there are very many shapes for the bison), diameter: 55 mm.*
98b *Variation, vertical type embroidery, horizontal for the buffalo.*
98c *Variation.*
98d *Variation, bison highlighted with white thread.*
98e *Variation, thin border around the buffalo, green back.*
98f *Variation, olive drab border.*

99 - 93rd Infantry Division

AC: activated 23 February 1942, organized 15 May 1942 at Fort Huachuca (Arizona), deactivated 3 February 1946 at Camp Stoneman (California). Unit comprising entirely of colored personnel, apart from field grade officers and generals.
A: 30 December 1918 by the AEF.
S: the French horizon blue helmet signifies the service of the four infantry regiments of the WW1 93rd Division (never totally formed) that saw service within French units in 1917-18.
C: 3 – 15 – 16.

99a *Standard WW2 manufacture.*
99b *Variation (diameter 60 mm).*
99c *Variation, the shape of the helmet is almost accurate, a great many variations can be seen from one manufacturer to another. The latter has 'German' type embroidery.*
99d *Variation 99a.*

TOUGH OMBRES!

The Story of the 90th Infantry Division

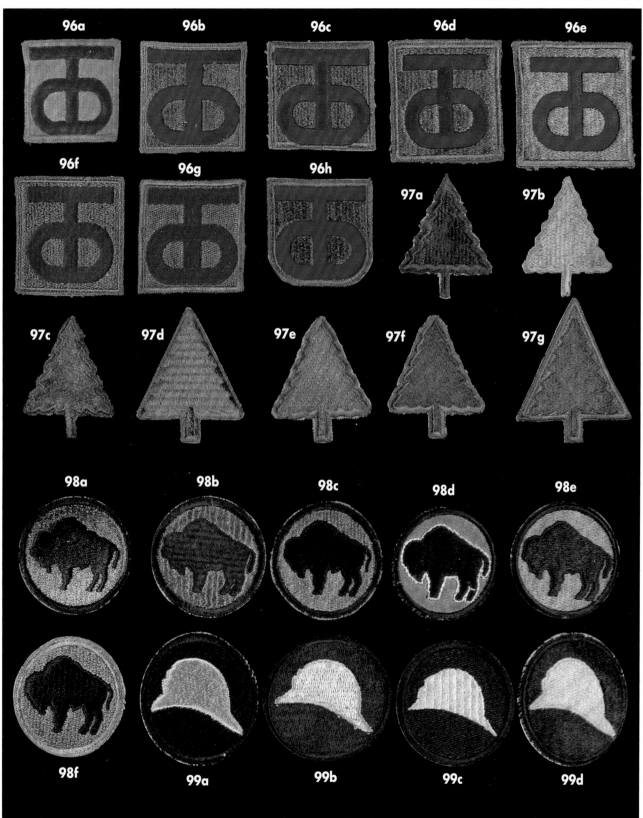

101 - 95th Infantry Division

AC: activated 4 September 1918 under the name of 95th Division. Organized in September 1918 at Camp Sherman (Ohio) and inactivated 21 December 1918 at the same place. Assigned 24 June 1921 to the Organized Reserve, organized in November 1921 in Oklahoma City (Oklahoma). Activated 15 July 1942, reorganized at Camp Swift (Texas) and re-designated 95th Infantry Division 1 August 1942. Inactivated 15 October 1945 at Camp Shelby (Mississippi).
A: 1st type: 28 August 1931. 2nd type: August 1942.
S: 1st type: letters O and K, for both the state from which the unit's men came from in 1921 and the Division's nickname. 2nd type: Roman numeral V and Arab numeral 9 for the numeric designation, along with the national colours. The V is also the initial for Victory, one of the unit's nicknames.
Nicknames: 'O.K. Division, Victory Division, Iron Men of Metz Division.'
C: 25 - 26 - 32 - 34.

101a *1st type patch: standard manufacture 1930-42, thin border around the letters (58 x 76 mm).*
101b *Variation, without border.*
101c *2nd type patch: standard WW2 manufacture, the two bars at the top of the V are above the 9 (55 x 76 mm).*
101d *Variation, the left bar of the V is behind the 9.*
101e *Variation.*
101f *Variation, red 9 borderd with white, the lower part of the V does not extend past the 9.*
101g *Variation, the V extends slightly past the lower part of the 9.*
101h *Variation.*
101i *Variation, olive drab border.*
101j *Variation.*

100 - 94th Infantry Division

AC: activated 24 June 1921 in the Organized Reserve as the 94th Division. Organized in November 1921 in Boston (Massachusetts). Activated 15 September 1942 at Fort Custer (Michigan) and re-designated 94th Infantry Division. Inactivated 7 February 1946 at Camp Kilmer (New Jersey).
A: there was a patch worn from July 1922 to May 1923 but it falls outside the scope of this publication.
1st type: 12 September 1923. 2nd type: 5 September 1942.
S: 1st type: silhouette of a Puritan as a reminder of the religious settlers in the region where the division was trained.
2nd type: numeric designation, no known meaning for the colours, black and gray. Nickname (unofficial): 'Neuf-Quatre Division' (in French).
C: 25 - 26 - 32 - 34.

100a *First type patch, 1925-30 manufacture, embroidered on gray felt (diam. 60 mm).*
100b *1925-40 manufacture, embroidered on olive drab wool, black back.*
100c *1930-40 manufacture, embroidered on dark gray felt, thin black twill to reverse.*
100d *1935-42 manufacture.*
100e *Variation, olive drab border and back, note the closed collar.*
100f *2nd type patch, standard WW2 manufacture (diam. 65 mm).*
100g *Variation.*
100h *Variation, the gray edge is no longer present on the right side.*
100i *Variation.*
100j *Variation, black border, embroidery known as German type.*

Above.
Germany 29 January 1945, Pfc Carl Aarmow of the 302nd Infantry wears the 94th Infantry Division patch on the shoulder.
(National Archives)

100a   100b   100c   100d   100e

100f   100g   100h   100i   100j

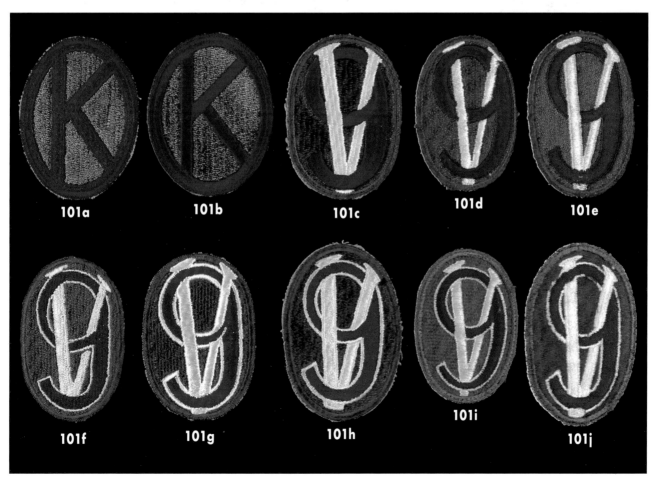

101a   101b   101c   101d   101e

101f   101g   101h   101i   101j

102 - 96th Infantry Division

AC: activated 5 September 1918 as the 96th Division, organized 20 October 1918 at Camp Wadsworth (South Carolina) and inactivated 7 January 1919 at the same place. Assigned 24 June 1921 to the Organized Reserve. Activated 15 August 1942, reorganized at Camp Adair (Oregon) as the 96th Infantry Division. Inactivated 3 February 1946 at Camp Anza (California).
A: 14 February 1927.
S: the two squares symbolize Oregon and Washington State where the unit's men first came from in WW1. The white and blue were the successive colours of the infantry; also, white is the symbol of purity and blue that of courage.
C: 13▲ - 19.

102a *Standard WW2 manufacture, white back (75 x 50 mm)*
102b *Variation, green back, thin border around the squares.*

103 - 97th Infantry Division

AC: activated 5 September 1918 under the name of 97th Division, organized 26 September 1918 at Camp Cody (New Mexico) and inactivated 22 December 1918 at the same place. Assigned 24 June 1921 to the Organized Reserve, organized in December 1921 in Manchester (New Hampshire). Activated 25 February 1943, reorganized at Camp Swift (Texas) and re-designated 97th Infantry Division. Inactivated 31 March 1946 in Japan.
A: 18 October 1922.
S: the three tips of the trident symbolize the states from which the division's men came from when it was reorganized in the nineteen twenties (Maine, New Hampshire and Vermont), along with the traditional infantry colours.
C: 26.

103a *Standard WW2 manufacture (50 x 60 mm).*
103b *Variation, thinner trident.*
103c *Variation*
103d *European made, chain stitch embroidery on blue twill, reinforced with brown twill to reverse.*
103e *Variation, silver bullion embroidery on very light blue felt, reinforced to reverse with glued white twill.*

104 - 98th Infantry Division

AC: activated 23 July 1918 under the name of 98th Division, organized in October 1918 at Camp McClellan (Alabama), inactivated in November 1918 at the same place. Assigned 26 June 1921 to the Organized Reserve, organized 18 August in Syracuse (New York). Activated 15 September 1942, reorganized at Camp Breckinridge (Kentucky) as the 98th Infantry Division. Inactivated 16 February 1946 in Japan.
A: 20 December 1922. *SP.*
S: the blue and orange colours are a reminder of the House of Nassau that administered New Amsterdam (later New York), the area where the unit was organized in the 1920s.
The Iroquois head is a reminder of this Indian nation's homeland, the five feathers symbolize the main tribes (Cayugas, Mohawks, Oneidas, Onondagas and Senegas). *SENECAS !*
Some sources surmise that the face is that of the Iroquois chief Hiawatha. *IROQUOIS DIV.*
C: Pacific Theatre without inscription.

104a *Standard WW2 manufacture (55 x 74 mm).*
104b *Variation.*
104c *Variation.*
104d *Variation, double orange border.*
104e *Variation. Note that there are many variations in the shape of the face and shades of orange.*
104f *WW2 patch, embroidery known as German, red face and border.*

105 - 99th Infantry Division

AC: activated 23 June 1918 under the name of 99th Division, organized in October 1918 at Camp Wheeler (Georgia), inactivated in November 1918 at the same place. Assigned 28 June 1921 to the Organized Reserve. Activated 15 November 1942, reorganized at Camp Van Dorn (Mississippi) as the 99th Infantry Division. Inactivated 27 September 1945 at Camp Patrick Henry (Virginia).
A: 21 May 1923.
S: the black shield symbolizes the steel manufacturing region of Pennsylvania, the checkerboard is from William Pitt's coat of arms, the founder of Pittsburgh, the nine blue and white squares (infantry colours) for the numeric designation. Nickname: 'The Checkerboard Division.'
C: 25 - 26 - 34.

105a *Standard WW2 manufacture (58 x 62 mm).*
105b *Variation, vertical black embroidery.*
105c *Variation, green back.*
105d *Variation, inverted checkerboard beginning with a blue square.*
105e *Variation (72 x 72 mm).*

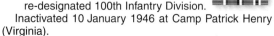
106f

106 - 100th Infantry Division

AC: activated 28 July 1918 as the 100th Division, organized in October 1918 at Camp Bowie (Texas) and inactivated 30 November 1918 at the same place. Assigned 24 June 1921 to the Organized Reserve. Activated 15 November 1942, reorganized at Fort Jackson (South Carolina) and re-designated 100th Infantry Division. Inactivated 10 January 1946 at Camp Patrick Henry (Virginia).
A: 29 May 1923.
S: numeric designation, infantry blue shield. Nickname: 'The Century Division.'
C: 25 - 26 - 34.

106a *Standard WW2 manufacture (50 x 63 mm).*
106b *Variation, green back.*
106c *Variation, embroidery known as 'German' type.*
106d *Variation.*
106e *Variation, inverted number colours.*
106f *Above, European manufacture, vertical background embroidery, silver and gold bullion embroidery, all on black wool, thick red reinforcing twill to reverse.*

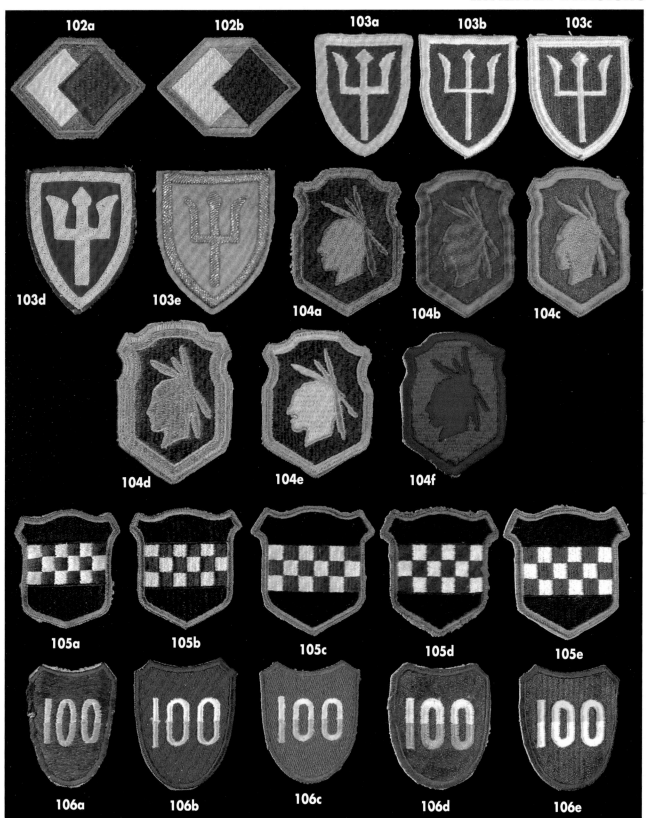

102a 102b 103a 103b 103c

103d 103e 104a 104b 104c

104d 104e 104f

105a 105b 105c 105d 105e

106a 106b 106c 106d 106e

107a   107b

107c   107d

107- 101st Airborne Division

AC: activated 23 July 1918 as the 101st Division, [image of ribbon] organized 2 November 1918 at Camp Shelby (Mississippi), inactivated 11 December 1918 at the same place. Assigned 24 June 1921 to the Organized Reserve. Activated at Camp Claiborne (Louisiana) as the 101st Airborne Division 15 August 1942, inactivated 30 November 1945 in France.

A: 1st type: November 1922. 2nd type: 23 May 1923. 'Airborne' tab authorized 28 August 1942.

S: 1st type: the shape of the shield is a reminder of the Civil War's Iron Brigade, the white eagle's head is that of Old Abe, the mascot of the 8th Wisconsin Volunteers regiment, the six feathers at the base of the head represent the six military districts of this state. The meaning of the crown of flames under the head is unknown.

2nd type: the shield and eagle's head remain, the flames are deleted. The relation between the reserve division of 1920-40 and the airborne division was only officially recognized in January 1950 when the 101st was reactivated. The tongue in the eagle's beak officially changed from white to red when the division became an airborne unit, but the reason remains unknown. The red tongue, however, could be seen well before this date.

C: 25 - 26 - 30s - 34▲.

107a *1st type: 1922-23 manufacture, white and yellow felt sewn onto black felt, white tongue (100 x 90 mm).*
107b *Variation, blue felt with merrowed border, the same type exists with a red tongue (78 x 80 mm).*
107c *2nd model/1st type: 1930-42. There are a great many variations in the design of the head, eye, beak and tongue (68 x 65 mm).*
107d *Variation, white tongue. This rare and much sought after patch has resulted in many reproductions, some of which are of the 3rd type (Airborne tab attached) which did not exist. These copies, when they are not just straightforward recently made patches, are altered red tongue patches, the latter having been removed and replaced by new white thread, the colour tone of which does not correspond to the white embroidery of the rest of the motif (57 x 60 mm).*
107e *2nd model/2nd type (1942-45): red tongue, separate tab (60 x 62 mm).*
107f *Variation, shorter tab (60 x 64 mm).*
107g *Variation, long tab, tongue totally absent.*
107h *Variation, green back for shield and tab, the latter being stitched at two points to the shield.*
107i *Variation.*
107j *Variation, embroidered shield on black twill with merrowed border, long tab, embroidered with yellow border.*
107k *European made, probably French, chain stitch embroidery on black wool (note the yellow eye); long tab, cotton embroidery on black wool, light reinforcing black twill to reverse.*
107l *WW2 British made, on black wool, merrowed border; short tab also embroidered on black wool.*
107m *Variation of 107l, black reinforcing twill to reverse; tab with thin white gauze to reverse and merrowed border.*

The Kid's lost treasure

I met Claude[1] during a militaria fair at the end of the nineteen seventies, he was 45 years old and already very ill. I told him of my great interest for American patches and he told me about his childhood during the war. His mother ran a millinery shop in Auxerre, his father worked on the railroads and was part of a resistance network.

The 101st Airborne Division was stationed around Auxerre in 1945, the return to the United States was not far off and many GI's went to Claude's mother's to have new patches sewn to their uniforms.

There was also a photographer's studio next door which was also busy as the GI's wished to immortalize their final weeks in Europe. Claude was only ten years old and soon became the mascot of the paratroopers who nicknamed him 'kid'. To keep up with demand, Claude's mother ordered 101st shoulder patches from a local manufacturer of sport and tourism patches.

Claude did not know the name of the town where this manufacturer was established, but did remember well that these patches were sewn onto black felt, which rendered them somewhat fragile, but they were very popular with the soldiers. This very particular type of patch (fig 113q on the plate) is often identified as being 1950s made, or even later. However, it can be seen fairly often on the right sleeve of veterans (as a Combat patch) as well as the left sleeve of soldiers wearing the discharge insignia.

The shop also managed to procure Distinguished Unit Citations from the US quartermasters. These badges came in boxes of 500, a box that would become Claude's treasure chest. His mother also sold parachute qualification badges, also French made[2], upon which she attached gold Croix de Guerre ribbon stars for the campaign stars. Claude remembered that his mother also made many 'ovals' in various colours, as worn under the metal paratrooper wings.

Claude had kept one of each but also traded several later with his schoolmates.

Sadly all of this was lost throughout the years as he moved. When we met he only had two patches left, one of which he gave to me and which is seen opposite, as well as a metal qualification badge. There were no photos left, only his childhood memories. 'Claude' left us too soon, a few months after we met, and this story is dedicated to his memory.

1. The name has been changed to protect his anonymity.
2. Which we will show in a future book.

107n *2nd model/3rd type, 1942-45: attached tab, embroidered at the same time as the shield (60 x 85 mm).*
107o *Variation, black back (63 x 85 mm).*
107p *Variation, the black base twill is visible between the shield and the tab (62 x 82 mm).*
107q *1945 French manufacture (see sidebar opposite), black velvet, thin white gauze to reverse, detailed head, black separation between head and beak, black merrowed edge (63 x 64 mm).*
107r *WW2 European manufacturer, black twill visible between the shield and the tab, black separation between the head and beak (70 x*

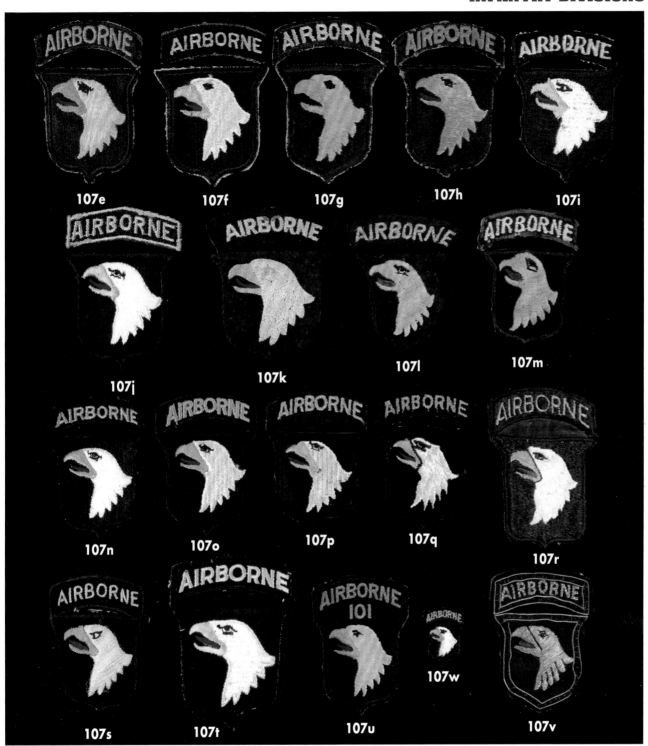

107e   107f   107g   107h   107i

107j

107k

107l

107m

107n   107o   107p   107q   107r

107s   107t   107u   107w   107v

100 mm).

107s *WW2 European made, maybe British, embroidered on black wool, thin white gauze to reverse, black inside border around the shield and the tab.*

107t *WW2 European made, embroidered on black twill, white reinforcing twill to reverse, black merrowed border, white edge around the head.*

107u *European made, no explanation has ever been found for this type… (60 x 83 mm)*

107v *European made (or American tailor made?), black twill, cotton embroidery (tongue), gilt and silver bullion embroidery.*

107w *Small size patch for the garrison cap or service coat and wool jacket lapel, non regulation American manufacture.*

109 - 103rd Infantry Division

AC: activated in November 1921 in the Organized Reserve as 103rd Division. Reorganized and re-designated 103rd Infantry Division 15 November 1942 at Camp Claiborne (Louisiana). Inactivated in November 1945 in Germany.

A: 14 October 1922.

S: the cactus symbolizes the southwest of the United States (Arizona-Colorado-New Mexico), from where the division's men came from when it was organized in 1921. In the inter-war period, the part of the patch beneath the cactus was in various colours according to the branch of service, thus leading to fifteen different patches. Nickname: 'Cactus Division.'

C: 25 - 26 - 34.

109a&b *1930-40 manufacture, the lower part of the patch is in the colours of the branch of service, blue here for the Infantry (a), maroon and white for the Medical dept. (b). Cotton embroidery on yellow wool, these were probably no longer worn during WW2 (diam. 63 mm).*
109c *Standard WW2 patch, there are numerous variations in colour tones from one manufacturer to another.*
109d *Variation*
109e *Variation*
109f *European made, without doubt German, cotton embroidery, olive drab edge, reinforced to the reverse with glued black paper (diameter 65 mm).*

110 - 104th Infantry Division

AC: activated 24 June 1921 in the Organized Reserve as the 104th Division, organized 7 October 1921 in Salt Lake City (Utah). Reorganized 15 September 1942 at Camp Adair (Oregon) and re-designated 104th Infantry Division. Inactivated 20 December 1945 at Camp San Luis Obispo (California).

A: 16 August 1924.

S: the timberwolf symbolizing cohesiveness of the pack, the rigors of life in the western states, the region from which the men came from when the division was organized in the nineteen twenties, but also tenacity in pursuing its prey, the unity of the objective.

C: 26 - 32 -34.

110a *1935-40 manufacture, light green base (diam. 55 mm). Note that there are many variations of green as well as the shape and embroidery of the timberwolf, depending on manufacturers.*

108 - 102nd Infantry Division

AC: activated 24 June 1921 in the Organized Reserve, under the name of 102nd Division, organized in November 1921 in Saint Louis (Missouri). Activated 15 September 1942, reorganized at Camp Maxey (Texas) and re-designated 102nd Infantry Division. Inactivated 12 March 1946 at Camp Kilmer (New Jersey).

A: 24 March 1923 (the previous insignia, a dog's head, worn from July 1922 to March 1924, does not fall within the cope of this book).

S: the initials O and Z of the Ozark mountains, a range in the area where the division trained in 1921. Nickname: 'Ozark Division.'

C: 26 - 34.

108a *Standard WW2 manufacture, thin border around the letters and rounded arch (diam. 68 mm).*
108b *Variation, thin letters.*
108c *Variation.*
108d *Variation.*

108a 108b 108c 108d 109a

109b 109c 109d 109e 109f

110a 110b 110c 110d 110e

110f 110g 110h 110i

110b *Variation.*
110c *Standard WW2 manufacture, medium green base, olive drab border (diam. 65 mm).*
110d *Variation, thin border around the timberwolf's head.*
110e *Variation.*
110f *Variation, horizontal embroidery.*
110g *Variation, very dark green base.*
110h *Variation, horizontal embroidery.*
110i *European made, medium green wool, note the eye and shape of the ear, the thin border around the head. Reverse reinforced with glued stock. Diameter 85 mm, a type no doubt designed to be worn on the flight jacket of artillery observation pilots.*

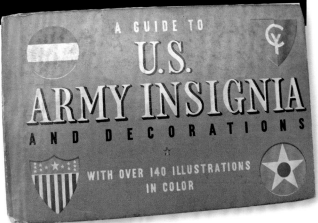
A GUIDE TO
U.S.
ARMY INSIGNIA
AND DECORATIONS
WITH OVER 140 ILLUSTRATIONS IN COLOR

"THE HUNGRY & SICK"

III - 106th Infantry Division

AC: activated 5 May 1942, organized 15 March 1943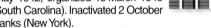
at Fort Jackson (South Carolina). Inactivated 2 October
1945 at Camp Shanks (New York).
A: 4 January 1943.
S: the lion's head symbolizes strength and the will to win, along with
the national colours. The blue also represents the infantry and the red
the artillery that supports it, the two main components of the division.
Nickname: 'Golden Lion Division.'
C: 5 - 26 - 34.

111a *Standard WW2 manufacture (diam. 64 mm). Note that there are a
great many variations in the shape of the head, its detailing and colour
tones from one manufacturer to another.*
111b *Variation*
111c *Variation.*
111d *Variation.*
111e *Variation, embroidery known as 'German' type.*

112 - Philippine Division

AC: activated 8 June 1921 at Fort McKinley, formed
with Philippine soldiers under the command of American officers. It took the number 12 on 6 April 1946 and was deactivated when the Philippines gained their independence on 30 April
1947. Although it did not exist after 9 April 1942 following its surrender
to Japanese troops, it was considered to be a 'captured unit,' a unique
status during the war.
A: 8 July 1922.
S: head of a water buffalo (Carabao), a very common animal in the Philippines, a reminder of where the division trained; the red and yellow colours
are those of Spanish royalty, the former colonial ruler of the archipelago.
C: 18.

112a *1920-25 manufacture, two pieces of felt sewn together (62 x 72 mm).
Note that there are numerous variations in the shape of the buffalo head
from one manufacturer to another.*
112b *Variation (75 x 82 mm).*
112c *1925-40 manufacture, embroidered on red felt, thin white gauze to
reverse.*
112d *Variation, two pieces of twill sewn together.*
112e *Variation, very thin red twill, note the eyes detailed in black.*
112f *Standard WW2 patch. This was not probably worn much before the
surrender in April 1942, it was worn as a combat patch on the right sleeve
by the rare survivors of this unit which was wiped out by the Japanese.*
112g *Variation.*
112h *Variation, olive drab border.*
112i *Variation, green back.*

113 - Americal Division

AC: activated 24 May 1942, organized 27 May 1942
in New Caledonia. Inactivated 12 December 1945.
Its origins go back to the War Department Task Force 6814 formed on 14 January 1942, and took the name of Americal Division
(contraction of America and Caledonia) upon activation. The division
took the number 23 when it was reactivated in the nineteen fifties.
A: 20 December 1943.
S: The four white stars symbolize the Southern Cross constellation,
visible where the division trained, along with the infantry colours.
C: 11 - 13 - 16 - 20▲.

113a *Standard WW2 manufacture (54 x 68 mm).*
113b *Variation (47 x 66 mm).*
113c *Variation, note that the left star has disappeared, no doubt
a manufacturer's error.*
113d *Variation of 113b, light blue base.*
113e *Embroidered on blue twill, flat edge, probably theatre made in New
Caledonia or Australia.*

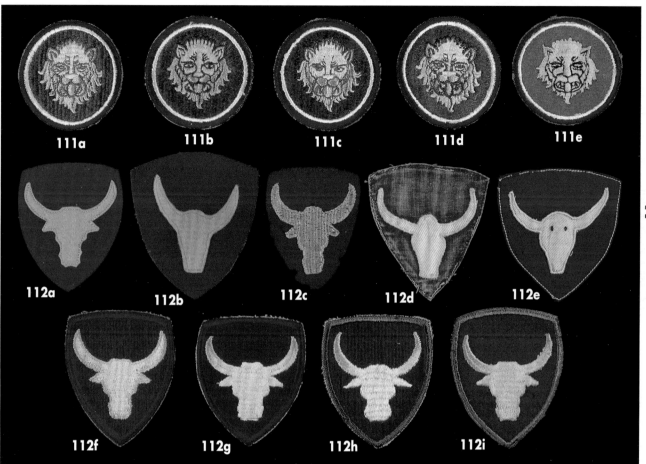

111a   111b   111c   111d   111e

112a   112b   112c   112d   112e

112f   112g   112h   112i

Previous page, top.
In Japan, shortly before returning to the USA late in 1945, these fighting men of the Americal Division receive the Purple Heart medal from the hands of an officer. The lieutenant, in the khaki summer uniform, wears the divisional patch on his shirt sleeve.
(National Archives via Jon Gawne)

the 106th

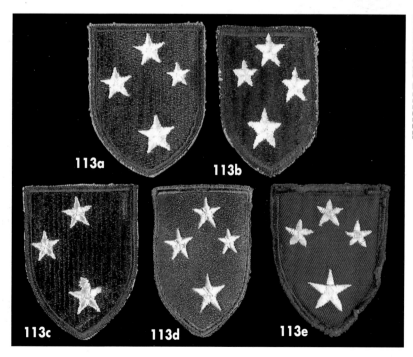

113a   113b

113c   113d   113e

81

NO ARMORED————!

INDEX

Series editor Philippe Charbonnier.
Design and layout by Matthieu Pleissinger. Translated from the French by Lawrence Brown.

Histoire & Collections
SA au capital de 182 938,82 €
5, avenue de la République
F-75541 Paris Cédex 11
Tel : +33(1) 40 21 18 20 / Fax : +33(1) 47 00 51 11
www.histoireetcollections.com

This book has been designed, typed, laid-out and processed by *Histoire & Collections* on fully integrated computer equipment.

Printed by Calidad Grafica, Spain, European Union.
September 2013.